SCOTTISH FIRST NAMES

GAIL DIXON-SMITH

Robinson
LONDON

Robinson Publishing Ltd

7 Kensington Church Court

London W8 4SP

A copy of the British Cataloguing in Publication Data for this title is
available from the British Library

ISBN 1-84119-032-2

Printed and bound in the E.C.

CONTENTS

INTRODUCTION

A PERSON'S FIRST NAME has always been a badge of cultural identity. A name may have linguistic variants, and these usually indicate the bearer's nationality: for example, John (English), Jean (French), Hans (German), Giovanni (Italian), Juan (Spanish), Ivan (Russian), or Iain (Scots).

Very rarely, it seems, is a name chosen on the basis of its meaning. Names almost always belong to a language more ancient than that spoken by their owners. Consequently, the meaning of a name is often obscured in a language other than the modern language spoken by the owner. Names can also be imported from another nation and adapted to the languages of those that use them.

In Scotland certain names are associated with particular clans. Scotland's history has been influenced by many factors, not least the division of the country by language, with the Gaelic-speaking population settling mainly in the Highlands from the fifth century onwards. Some of the Scottish Gaelic names currently in use are associated with pre-Christian myths.

The Gaelic custom of naming children was, until recently, very traditional. The most common practice was to name the eldest son and daughter after their paternal grandfather and maternal grandmother, then the second son and daughter after their maternal grandfather and paternal grandmother. This could be varied in that the first son and daughter could be named after the maternal grandfather and paternal grandmother.

In most European languages more than half of the more usual names owe their importance to Christian tradition. This influence in Scotland is very strong. Religion has played a major role in shaping its history. These common Christian names usually have numerous cognates in other European languages: for example, David, John and Sarah.

Some Christian names have very ancient origins, in a pre-Christian past; Malcolm, from the Gaelic, is but one example. St Columba, the Irish missionary, who brought Christianity to the Gaels and Picts in Scotland, is commemorated in the names Calum and Malcolm.

Before the mid-eighteenth century it was rare for people to have more than one Christian name. Thereafter, however, the introduction of a second Christian name gradually changed the naming pattern. It brought in the custom of including a surname from the mother's side of the family as a first name, with a child being christened with the mother's maiden name: for example, Douglas, Fraser or Keith.

Many of the most common masculine names of Germanic origin used in Britain today owe their importance to having been royal names: Robert in Scotland, for example.

By transferred usage, ordinary words, topographic terms and place names have also contributed to the wealth of Scottish first names.

Sometimes names have been used by people who may be only vaguely aware of the names' derivations from Scottish or Irish Gaelic or from Welsh. Today, it has become fashionable to indicate family roots or country of origin by giving children more unusual names. In Scotland names of Gaelic origin have become more popular. In this way, some of the Scottish Gaelic names of the Highlands and Islands survive, and tradition lives on.

BOYS' FIRST NAMES

BOYS' NAMES

Achaius. *See* HECTOR

Adaidh. *See* ADAM

Adair [ad-air]
Meaning: 'fortunate spear' in Anglo-Saxon.
This is an early Scottish pronunciation of EDGAR. It became a surname but in recent times, especially in Scotland, it has been revived as a first name.
Famous name: Red Adair, oil fire fighter.

Adam [ad-im]
Meaning: 'red earth' in Hebrew.
The first time that the name Adam comes to light again after biblical times is among the Celtic Christians of Scotland and Ireland. It was possibly first adopted according to the Gaelic fashion as the ecclesiastical name most resembling the native name Aedh ('fire').

In medieval Scotland, Edom was taken to represent a variant of Adam. Again, a biblical influence as Edom was the byname of Esau, given to him because he sold his birthright for a bowl of red lentil soup. Adamnan (the diminutive of Adam) was a seventh-century abbot of Iona and his country's historian. He wrote an account of the Holy Land which long served as a guidebook for pilgrims.

Adam became a national Christian name, and the family who used it most were the Gay Gordons. The Gordons had their Scottish origins in Berwickshire and maintained estates there for three centuries. Sir Adam de Gordon was one of the ambassadors who conveyed the 1320 Declaration of National Independence to the Pope. For this, Bruce granted him lands in Aberdeenshire and their chief was often called 'Cock of the North'.

Variant spellings: Adie, Edom
Diminutives: Addie, Addy, Adkin, Atty, Edie, Yiddie
Gaelic cognates: Adhamh, Adaidh
Famous names: Adam Faith, pop singer; Adam Thorpe, novelist.

Adhamh. *See* ADAM

Adie. *See* ADAM

Adi. *See* AIDAN

Aeneas. *See* ANGUS

Aidan [ai-din]
Meaning: derived from the Gaelic diminutive word for 'little fiery one'.
Aidan was a ruler of the early Scottish kingdom of Dalriada, and was consecrated as king of the Scots by Columba, the earliest recorded ordination in Scotland.

St Aidan, a monk of Iona, was sent by King Oswald to establish a monastery on the island of Lindisfarne, and eventually became Bishop of the Angles. He was known as the Apostle of Northumberland and his emblem is a stag.

Variant spellings: Aiden, Adin
Gaelic cognate: Eadan

Ailean. *See* ALAN

Aili. *See* ALASDAIR

Ailig. *See* AINSLIE; *see also* ARNSLEY

Ailpein. *See* ALPIN

Aindrea. *See* ANDREW

Ainslie [ains-lee]
Meaning: Old English for 'hermitage' or 'wood'.
Originally a surname, the name is now used in Scotland as a first name for both boys and girls.
Variant spellings: Aynslie, Ainsley
Famous name: Ainslee Harriott, television chef.

Alan [al-in]
Meaning: Celtic origin, 'harmony'; or Latin origin, 'cheerful'. *Ail* meant 'rock' in Gaelic.
The mythical Greek poet Olen is said to have been the first writer of hymns in hexameter and the name is said to mean 'flute-player'. This is probably the origin of the Breton name Alan.

Before the Norman Conquest, an Alan (of Norman or Breton parentage) lived in Britain and in the reign of Henry I an Alan held Oswestry. His grandson, also Alan, became High Steward of Scotland – progenitor of the clan Stuart and the Alan and Allens in Scotland. The use of the name has led to such surnames as MacAllen and Callan.

Variant spellings: Allan, Allen, Alyn
Gaelic cognates: Ailean. It is also possible that the Gaelic name Aikan derived from *ail*, meaning rock.
Famous names: Alan Bates, actor; Alan Rickman, actor; Alan Moorehead, author, Allan Ramsay, eighteenth-century painter; Alan Titchmarsh, presenter of television gardening programmes.

Alasdair [al-as-dair]
Meaning: 'defender of men'.
This is the Gaelic form of Alexander. In Scotland both Alexander and Alasdair are used as distinct names.

In Greek mythology, the name Alexander was said to have been given to Paris for repelling robbers from the flocks.

The most famous bearer of the name is the Macedonian king, Alexander the Great (356–322 BC). He was appointed regent when he was only sixteen years old and became king before he was twenty. He soon conquered Persia, Asia Minor and Babylon.

The name was associated with sainthood in the fifth century. A young Roman noble called Allexius was determined to live a monastic life. On the day that his parents had decreed as his wedding day, he fled to a monastery, where he remained for seventeen years. He came home disguised as a beggar and for another seventeen years he lived on scraps from his father's kitchen and made himself known to his parents only as he was dying.

The name was imported to Scotland with other Greek names by Margaret Atheling, who learnt of them in the Hungarian court where she was brought up. Her son was Alexander I, king of Scotland in the twelfth century and the name remains very popular in Scotland.

Alexander Selkirk was the Scottish sailor whose experience as a castaway gave Defoe the inspiration for *Robinson Crusoe*.
Variant spellings: Alistair, Alaster, Alistar, Alister, Allistair
Diminutives: Alec, Alick, Alex, Aleck, Allie, Ally, Andy, Sandy, Saunder
Gaelic cognates: Sandaidh of Sandy, Aili of Ally, Ailig of Alec, Alick
Famous names: Sir Alexander Fleming, discoverer of penicillin; Alexander Graham Bell, inventor of the telephone; Alex Hill, television weather presenter; Alec Guinness, actor; Alec Stewart, England cricket captain; Alistair Maclean, novelist; Sandy Lyle, golfer; Alasdair Gray, author; Alastair Sim, actor.

Alaster. *See* ALASDAIR

Alban [alb-in]
Meaning: 'white' in Latin and Celtic.
St Alban, a Romano-Briton, was the first British martyr. He lived in what is now the city of St Albans. During Diocletian's persecution he gave shelter to a fleeing Christian and was beheaded for this charity in AD 209. St Alban's Abbey stands on the site of his execution.

St Albanus, or St Abban, was an Irish Bishop who was consecrated by St Patrick and whose name is probably the source of the Scottish Christian name Albany. Deriving ultimately from the Gaelic word *alp*, meaning 'rock' or 'mountain', it could also be an allusion to Scotland. The Duke of Albany was the Scottish title of the future James II of England.
Variant spelling: Albany

Alec. *See* ALEXANDER

Alexander. *See* ALASDAIR

Alistair. *See* ALASDAIR

Allan. *See* ALAN

Allen. *See* ALAN

Allie. *See* ALASDAIR

Allister. *See* ALASDAIR

Alpin [al-pin]
Meaning: possibly related to the Latin for 'white'.
Kenneth MacAlpin, the son of an Ailpen, succeeded to the throne of Dalriada. The kingdom was menaced by Norsemen sailing south through the Hebrides. King Kenneth, from the central Highlands of Scotland, set out to consolidate as much as he could of the remaining Celtic territories, setting himself up as the first king of both the Picts and the Scots.

The name was adopted by the early Scottish settlers, but survives mainly in the form of such surnames as Macalpine and Elphin.
Gaelic cognate: Ailpein

Alyn. *See* ALAN

Alyster. *See* ALASDAIR

Amhlainbh. *See* ANLAY

Andreas. *See* ANDREW

Andrew [an-drew]
Meaning: 'manly' in Greek.
Andreas, the Galilean fisherman who was the brother of Simon Peter, was one of the twelve apostles. He was martyred at Patras, in Achaia, and some of his relics were carried to Scotland in the fourth century.

St Andrew became the patron saint and knightly champion of Scotland. This is partly why the name became one of the most popular Christian names in the country.

The early association of the name with Scotland is reflected in surnames such as Anderson, Andrews, Andison, Drew, Gillanders, and Macandrew.
Variant spelling: Andreas (the Latin form).
Diminutives: Andy, Andie, Dandie, Dandy, Drew
Gaelic cognates: Anndra, Aindrea
Famous names: Andrew Carnegie, philanthropic millionaire; Andrew, Duke of York; Drew, son of Charlemagne.

Andy. *See* ALASDAIR and ANDREW

Angus [ang-gus]
Meaning: from the Celtic *oino-gustu-s*, 'one choice'.
Angus, in various forms, has been known in Scotland for centuries. Aanghas was supposedly the name of an ancient Celtic god. Aonghas or Oengus was the name of the Pictish king who had overlordship of the Scots in the eighth century.

Aonghus Turimleach was one of three Irish brothers who invaded Scotland in the sixth century. They brought with them the Stone of Scone, or Stone of Destiny, on which all Scottish kings were afterwards crowned.

It was sent south to England after the defeat by Edward I in 1296, and used to lie under the Coronation Chair in Westminster, but has now been returned to Scotland.

Angus held the kingdom of Moray, in northern Pictland, when in 1124 David arrived from England as the new king of Scotland. In 1130 a battle was fought between the men of Scotland and Moray. Moray was defeated and Angus was killed. David made generous concessions to the true heirs, making the nephew of Angus, Earl of Fife.

Clan MacDonell have used the name Angus since the fifteenth century.

Variant spelling: Aeneas

Gaelic cognate: Aonghas

Famous names: Angus Ogilvie, husband of Princess Alexandra; Angus Lennie, Scottish actor; Angus Deayton, television presenter.

Anndra. *See* ANDREW

Anton. *See* ANTONY

Antony [an-tun-ee]

Meaning: a Roman name which might mean 'priceless'.

Antony was the name of a Roman family, the most famous member of which was Mark Antony, renowned for his love of Cleopatra.

During the reign of Antonius Pius, a benevolent Roman emperor, the Antonine Wall was built in Scotland to define the northern boundary of the Roman Empire. St Antony, the 3rd- to 4th-century Egyptian hermit, is regarded as the founder of monasticism. He created his own cult, gathering a community of hermits around him in his old age.

The temptation of St Antony was a favourite subject in

medieval art. He was regarded as the patron saint of swineherds, and a St Antony, or Tantony, pig was a name for the smallest pig in the litter.

Antony became a common name in Scotland from the twelfth century and the popularity of the name was further increased by the fame of St Anthony of Padua (1195–1231), who is believed to help people find lost things.

Variant spellings: Anton (in Middle Scots); Anthony (from the late sixteenth century onwards).

Diminutives: Nanty, Tony

Famous names: Anthony Hopkins, actor; Antony Andrews, actor; Antony Sher, actor; Tony Biar, British prime minister.

Aodh [ugh]
Meaning: 'fire' in Celtic.

Aodh is associated with HUGH because of the names' similar pronunciation. It was the name of two early kings of the Scottish kingdom of Dalriada.

The kingdom of Dalriada was built up by Irish invaders on land in the west of Scotland that had been owned by the Picts. Adamnan called it 'The Spine of Scotland', and it lay north of Strathclyde, stretching up to and beyond the Great Glen.

Aonghas. *See* Angus

Archibald [artch-ee-bald]
Meaning: 'excellent, noble and bold' in Old German.

Archie Armstrong was a jester that James I brought with him to England.

He figures in Sir Walter Scott's *Legend of Montrose*, the story of the campaign of 1644, in which the Highland clans rose in favour of Charles I under the generalship of the Earl of Montrose and defeated their opponents.

Variant spellings: Archie; Baldie.

Gaelic cognate: Gilleasbaig, which means 'servant of a bishop'. An accepted explanation is that this is due to the mistaken notion that *bald* in Archibald means hairless and the equivalent of the Gaelic *gille*, 'servant' or 'shaven one' or 'monk'.

Famous names: A.J. Cronin, author; Archie Gemmell, footballer.

Archie. *See* ARCHIBALD

Artair. *See* ARTHUR

Arthur [arth-er]

Meaning: possibly derived from 'bear' or 'stone' in Celtic, or 'valorous' in Old English.

A Roman clan bore the name Artorius; Tacitus mentions an Artoria Flacilla.

The name first appeared as Arturius in the thirteenth century, in Adamnan's *Life of St Columba*, where it is the name of an Irish prince killed in 596.

The Celtic hero King Artair (Arthur) was probably a leading figure in the resistance to the Anglo-Saxon invaders of what is now England.

Gaelic cognate: Artair

Famous names: Arthur Wellesley, Duke of Wellington; Arthur Ashe, tennis player; Arthur Askie, actor and comedian; Arthur Ransome, author.

Athol [ath-ol]
Meaning: 'new Ireland' in Gaelic.
Athol is the name of a district in Glen Garry and also a surname. The Murrays lived at Athol and the Dukes of Atholl were chiefs of the old Tullibardine branch. Athol has been used as a first name since 1870.
Variant spellings: Atholl, Athole

Augustine. *See* AUSTIN

Aulay [au-lee]
Meaning: Gaelic origin, representing an old Norse name, Anleifr, composed of elements meaning 'ancestor' and 'relics'. In turn this represents a Scandinavian name appearing as Olaf.

In an attempt to weaken Shetland's ties with Norway the islanders were encouraged to use Oliver as a substitute. Some parents have chosen to revert to Auley.

Both Aulay and Macaulay are occasionally used as first names in Scotland.
Gaelic cognate: Amhlaibh
Famous name: Macaulay Culkin, actor.

Austin [aus-tin]
Meaning: 'venerable' in Latin.
In the Middle Ages this was the ordinary spoken form of Augustine.

The name was made famous by St Augustine of Hippo, author of the *Confessions* and the *City of God*. Another St Augustine became the first archbishop of Canterbury.

The name is often used as a substitute for the Gaelic Uisdean in Scotland, due to the similarity in sound. Austin and Asten are common surnames.

Variant spelling: Austyn
Famous names: Austin Mitchell, MP; Austin Healey, rugby player

Aynslie. *See* AINSLIE

Baldie. *See* ARCHIBALD

Barclay [bark-lee]
Meaning: 'one who lived by the birch meadow' in Old English.
The name is almost certainly derived from Berkley, in Gloucestershire. It was taken to Scotland in the twelfth century by Walter de Berchelai, Chamberlain of Scotland.

Barnard. *See* BERNARD

Bartram [bar-tram]
Meaning: 'bright raven' in Teutonic.
This is the Scottish form of Bertram. St Bertichramnus was a seventh-century bishop of Mans.
Variant spellings: Bertrand, Bertram
Famous names: Bertrand Russell, philosopher; Bertram Mills, circus owner.

Bearnard. *See* BERNARD

Beathan [bee-thin]
Meaning: derived from the Celtic for 'offspring of life'.
Beathan is the Scottish form of Benjamin, a biblical name derived from the Hebrew meaning 'son of my right hand'. In the Old Testament, Benjamin was the youngest and favourite son of Jacob and Rachel.
  It was the name of the supposed first bishop of Mortlach. (Mortlach preceded Aberdeen as the ecclesiastical centre of Scotland.)
Diminutives: Ben, Benjy
Famous names: Benjamin Disraeli, politician.

Benjamin. *See* BEATHAN

Bernard [ber-nard]
Meaning: 'brave as a bear' in Old German.
The name was introduced to Britain by the Normans in the eleventh century. St Bernard of Montjoux (996–1081), patron saint of mountaineers, founded an order and built two rest houses for travellers at the top of two Alpine passes, now known as Great and Little St Bernard. St Bernard dogs were named after him.

St Bernard of Clairvaux (1090–1153) founded the Cistercian Order. Bernard was also the name of the abbot of Arbroath and chancellor of Scotland, who was credited as the author of the Declaration of Arbroath, a statement of the Scots' commitment to national independence, which they sent to the pope in 1320.
Variant spellings: Barnard, Bernhard
Gaelic cognate: Bearnard
Famous names: Bernhard Langer, golfer; George Bernard Shaw, playwright; Bernard Levin, journalist.

Bertram. *See* BARTRAM

Bertrand. *See* BARTRAM

Bhaltair. *See* WALTER

Blair [blair]
Meaning: 'plain, field, battlefield' or 'clearing in a wood' in Gaelic.
Once a Scottish surname, it is now also used as a first name.
Gaelic cognate: Blar

Boyd [boyd]

Meaning: 'yellow' in Celtic.

Probably describing the colour of hair, this is a well-known Scottish surname which is occasionally used as a first name. Robert, grandson of Alan Fitz Faald, was named Buidhe ('yellow') because of the colour of his hair, and is thought to be the founder of the Scottish Boyds.

Sir Robert Boyd was a staunch supporter of Robert the Bruce and one of the commanders at the Battle of Bannockburn in 1314.

Famous name: William Boyd, novelist.

Bruce [broos]

Meaning: originally from a French place name probably meaning 'brushwood thicket'.

It came to Britain as a surname after the Norman Conquest and is the transferred use of the Scottish surname of Robert the Bruce, liberator and king of Scotland. It is said that Robert the Bruce drew his inspiration after his defeat at Methven from the perserverance of a spider in repeatedly climbing up again after being knocked down. He went on to defeat the English at the Battle of Bannockburn in 1314.

Gaelic cognate: Brus

Buchan [buk-n]

Meaning: place name meaning 'little hut'.

This is a surname (the surname of the barons Tweedsmuir), now also used as a first name.

17

Cailean. *See* COLIN

Calum [ku-lum]
Meaning: Gaelic form of Columba, meaning 'dove'.
In the sixth century, St Columba left Ireland with twelve companions to found a monastery on Iona, off the west coast of Scotland, and converted the Pictish and Scottish inhabitants to Christianity. The dove is a symbol of purity, peace and the Holy Spirit; thus the name became popular with the early Christians.

In the Scottish Highlands, Callum is considered to be a form of Malcolm.
Variant spelling: Callum. *See* also MALCOLM

Cameron [kam-er-in]
Meaning: from the Gaelic for 'crooked nose'.
A Scottish clan name and surname, now used as a first name.

The clan Cameron, led by 'gentle Lochiel', were among the first supporters of Charles Stuart, the Young Pretender, better known as Bonnie Prince Charlie, and were decisively defeated at the Battle of Culloden (1746).
Gaelic cognate: Camran
Famous name: Cameron Mackintosh, theatre producer.

Campbell [kam-bil]
Meaning: from the Gaelic for 'crooked mouth'.
This is a Scottish clan name and surname now used as a first name.

The clan Campbell became infamous in Scottish history for their part in the massacre at Glencoe in 1692, when thirty-eight members of the clan MacDonald were treacherously murdered. Throughout history the chiefs combined their roles of Highland clan chiefs with a strong presence at court, which insured them a leading part in the affairs of Scotland, Great Britain and the Empire.

Camran. *See* CAMERON

Carmichael [karm-eye-kil]
Meaning: 'loved of Michael' in Gaelic, with special reference to the Archangel, St Michael.
The name has also become a surname. Cara ('friend') was sometimes prefixed to a saint's name by the Christian Gaels.

Carson [kar-sin]
Meaning: 'son of a marsh-dweller'.
This is a surname now used as a Christian name.
Famous name: Carson McCullers, author.

Cathal [kath-al]
Meaning: 'battle mighty' in Celtic.

Christopher [kris-ter-fu]
Meaning: from the Greek for 'one who carries Christ in his heart'.
St Christopher was an early Christian martyr who, according to legend, carried the Christ-child across a river. He is the patron saint of travellers and the sight of an image of St Christopher was thought to give protection from accidents.
Variant spellings: Crystal, Chrystal
Diminutives: Christie, Kit
Gaelic cognate: Crisdean
Famous names: Sir Christopher Wren, architect; Christopher

Columbus, navigator and explorer; Christopher Isherwood, novelist.

Clement [kle-mint]
Meaning: 'mild' or 'merciful'
St Clement was a disciple of St Paul and the first of the Apostolic Fathers. The name was also adopted by several popes.
Variant spellings: Clemens, Clemence
Gaelic cognate: Cliamain
Famous names: Clement Attlee, politician; Clement Freud, television chef.

Cliamain. *See* CLEMENT

Clyde [klyd]
This name was often given to people who lived on the banks of the River Clyde, which flows through Glasgow.

Coinneach. *See* KENNETH

Colin [kol-in]
Meaning: 'young dog' or 'youth' in Gaelic.
This is the anglicised form of the Gaelic name Cailean and is related to Columba (*see* CALUM). It was particularly favoured among the Campbells and the MacKenzies. Related to St Columba.
Variant spelling: Collin
Gaelic cognate: Cailean
Famous name: Colin Montgomery, golfer.

Coll [kol]
Meaning: derived from the Celtic for 'high'.

This is an anglicized form of the Gaelic name Colla. Both the MacDonalds and MacDougals claim descent from a Colla of the early fourth century, and Colla Ciotach ('left-handed Colla' or 'cunning Colla') was a leading MacDonald warrior of the sixteenth century.

Craig [kraig]
Meaning: 'rugged rock' in Gaelic.
This was originally a surname, especially for someone who lived near a steep or precipitous rock.
It is now also used as a first name.
Famous names: Craig Riche, television weather presenter.

Crawford [kraw-ford]
Meaning: 'ford where crows gather'.
The vast hill-district of Crawford, in Lanarkshire, was held by William de Lindsay of the Lindsay clan. This place name, which became a surname, is now also used as a first name.

Creighton [kry-ton]
Meaning: 'border village' in Gaelic.
The name is derived from the old barony of Crighton, in Midlothian. Once a surname, it is now also used as a first name.
Variant spellings: Crighton, Crichton

Crighton. *See* CREIGHTON

Crisdean. *See* CHRISTOPHER

Crystal. *See* CHRISTOPHER

Cuithbeirt. *See* CUTHBERT

Cuthbert [kuth-bert]
Meaning: composed of elements meaning 'famous, known, bright' in Old English.

St Cuthbert was a seventh-century Northumbrian shepherd boy, when the kingdom of Northumbria included England north of the Humber and Scotland nearly up to the Highlands. He became a monk at the monastery of Melrose, then prior, before he became abbot of Lindisfarne. After several years he felt called to a life of solitude, and returned to the small island of Farne. In 684, against his will, he was made bishop of Lindisfarne. In 686, he returned to Farne, where he died.

His feast day is 20 March. Kirkcudbright was named after him.
Diminutives: Cuddie, Cuddy
Gaelic cognate: Cuithbeirt

Cyrus. *See* GREIG

Daibhidh. *See* DAVID

Dallas [dal-las]
Meaning: 'water meadow'.
This was originally a surname, from the place name Dallas, in Elginshire. It is now also a first name.

Dandie. *See* ANDREW

David [day-vid]
Meaning: Hebrew for 'darling' or 'beloved'.
David was the greatest Israelite king. He became famous as a boy for killing the giant Philistine, Goliath, with his slingshot. As king of Judah and later of all Israel, he extended the power of the Israelites. He was also known as a poet, and many of the biblical psalms are attributed to him.

This is a particularly common name in Scotland. Two kings of this name ruled in Scotland in the twelfth and fourteenth centuries.

David I of Scotland established a form of central government, issued the first royal coinage and was canonized for his lavish donations to the church, causing James I of England to call him '*a sair* (sore) *saint for the crown*'. David II invaded England, was defeated and imprisoned for eleven years.
Gaelic cognate: Daibhdh
Diminutive: Davy
Famous names: David Livingstone, explorer; David McCallum, actor; David Hockney, artist; David Bowie, singer; Sir David Steele, politician.

Davy. *See* DAVID

Denham. *See* DENHOLM

Denholm [den-him]
Meaning: probably 'settlement in a valley'.
This place name in Roxburghshire became a Scottish surname. It is also used as a first name in Scotland.
Variant spelling: Denham
Famous name: Denholm Elliot, actor.

Derek [der-ick]
Meaning: from 'peoples' ruler' in German.
This name, a shortened version of Theodoric, was brought to Britain from Holland in the fifteenth century.
Variant spelling: Derrick
Famous name: Sir Derek Jacobi, actor.

Derick. *See* RODERICK

Derrick. *See* DEREK

Dhugall. *See* DOUGAL

Diarmid [jir-mut]
Meaning: 'freeman' in Celtic or 'without envy' in Gaelic.
Diarmid was a distinguished hero of the Feen, who had a beauty spot which made all the women fall in love with him. He fell in love with his uncle's wife and they ran away together. On discovering their hiding place his uncle ordered him to join the hunt for a huge and dangerous boar. Diarmid killed the beast. However, Diarmid, like Achilles, had a fatal spot in his foot. Remembering this, his uncle insisted that Diarmid measure the size of the boar by pacing along the huge dead beast. One of the bristles pierced his

foot and killed him. His wife was then forced to remarry Diarmid's uncle.

Variant spellings: Diarmaid, Diarmad, sometimes anglicized as Jeremiah or Jeremy.

Famous names: Jeremy Irons, actor; Jeremy Paxton, television presenter; Hugh MacDiarmid, poet and critic and founder of the National Party of Scotland.

Dick. *See* RICHARD

Domhnall. *See* DONALD

Donal. *See* DONALD

Donald [don-ald]
Meaning: 'proud' or 'world ruler' in Celtic.
This is a Scottish clan name and surname that is now also used as a first name.

Donald I is thought to have been the first Christian king of Scotland. Donald III (c. 1031–97) was twice deposed and also blinded and was the last king to be buried on Iona.
Variant spellings: Don, Donal
Diminutives: Don, Donny
Gaelic cognate: Domhnall
Famous names: Donald Campbell, world waterspeed record holder; Donald Sutherland, actor; Donny Osmond, musician.

Donnchadh. *See* DUNCAN

Dougal [doo-ghul]
Meaning: 'dark stranger' in Gaelic.
This was originally a name applied to Vikings. From ancient

times it has been a Highland name and, together with DONALD, served as a nickname that Lowlanders give to Highlanders. It was initally a surname, but is now used as a first name, mainly in the Highlands.

Variant spellings: Dugald, Dhugal, Dugal
Gaelic cognate: Dughall

Douglas [dug-las]
Meaning: 'dark water'.

This is a Scottish place name and surname that is now also used as a first name. The Douglases were the greatest family in medieval Scotland. Their founder, Black Douglas (1286–1330) invaded England, and ravaged and plundered many villages in the north. He died fighting the Moors in Spain on his way to the Crusades.

In 1421 a Scots army led by the Earl of Douglas defeated the English at Beauge and acquired the French Dukedom of Touraine.

Diminutives: Doug, Duggie
Gaelic cognate: Dughlas
Famous names: Douglas Fairbanks, actor

Drew. *See* ANDREW

Drummond [drum-ond]
Meaning: 'ridge' or 'high ground' in Gaelic.

This clan name and surname is derived from a place name, the parish of Drymen, near Loch Lomond. It has been linked with Scottish history since the thirteenth century, and is now also used as a first name.

The Drummond arms display the motto 'Going warily'.

Annabella Drummond became consort of Robert II, the first Stuart king.

Famous name: Drummond of Hawthornden (1585–1649), author.

Dubh. *See* DUFF

Duff [duff]
Meaning: 'dark' or 'black'.
Duff is the Scottish short form of various Gaelic compounds. Duff was originally a nickname for a person with dark hair or a swarthy complexion.

Dubh was the name of a Scottish-Pictish king who was killed in 967. The chiefs of the clan Macduff had the right of enthroning the Scottish king on the Stone of Destiny at Scone. Robert the Bruce was crowned king by a Macduff – Isabel, countess of Buchan – in 1306. Captured later by Edward I she was punished by being confined in a cage in public view at Berwick.

Macduff and his wife also feature in Shakespeare's *Macbeth*.
Gaelic cognate: Dubh

Dugald. *See* DOUGAL

Duggie. *See* DOUGLAS

Dughall. *See* DOUGAL

Dughlas. *See* DOUGLAS

Duncan [dun-can]
Meaning: 'brown soldier' or 'dark-skinned warrior' in Celtic.
St Duncan was a seventh-century abbot of Iona. The Scottish king Duncan I (1010–40) was murdered by his

cousin Macbeth. Duncan II (1060–94) was murdered by his uncle, Donald III, after ruling for only six months.

Gaelic cognate: Donnchadh

Famous names: Duncan Goodhew, swimmer; Duncan Grant, painter.

Eachann. *See* HECTOR

Eadan. *See* AIDAN

Ealair. *See* HILARY

Eamann. *See* EDMUND

Edgar [ed-gar]
Meaning: 'wealthy spear' in Old English.
Eadgar was king of the Scots from 1097 to 1107. The name became a surname in Scotland, later again being used as a first name.
Famous names: Edgar Allan Poe, author; Edgar Wallace, crime writer.
See also ADAIR

Edmund [ed-mund]
Meaning: from the Old English for 'happy protection'.
This is the Gaelic form of the English name Edmund.
St Edmund, king and martyr (841–869), the ruler of East Anglia, was murdered by the Danes and his body enshrined at Bury St Edmunds. Two English kings were called Edmund, Edmund the Magnificent and Edmund Ironside.
Gaelic cognate: Eamann
Famous names: Edmund Halley, astronomer; Sir Edmund Hillary, explorer and mountaineer.

Edom. *See* ADAM

Edward [ed-ward]
Meaning: derived from the Old English for 'rich guardian'.
Edward the Elder, son of Alfred the Great, was one of the

greatest of the West Saxon kings of England. Edward the Confessor founded Westminster Abbey and was canonized in 1611. Edward V was one of the two princes supposedly murdered on the instructions of their uncle, Richard III.

Variant spelling: Eudard

Gaelic cognate: Eideard

Famous names: Edward Lear, author; Edward Elgar, composer.

Eideard. *See* EDWARD

Eliot. *See* ELLIOT

Ellar [el-lar]
This is an anglicized form of a Gaelic name, referring to someone who was a butler or steward in a monastery.

Elliot [ell-ee-ot]
Meaning: possibly derived from the Old English for 'elf-ruler'.
This is a Border surname which is sometimes used as a first name in Scotland.

The origins of the Elliots is unclear; they appeared in the fifteenth century as the Ellots. They fought in the Battle of Flodden Field in Northumberland in 1513.

The Earl of Surrey, on behalf of Henry VIII, defeated James IV. Robert, their thirteenth chief, was killed on the field, along with James IV. Elliot is also the surname of the Earls of Minto.

Variant spellings: Eliot, Elliott

Famous name: Elliot Gould, actor.

Eoghann. *See* EWAN

Eosaph. *See* JOSEPH

Errol [er-rol]
Meaning: from 'wandering' or 'wanderer' in Latin.
A Scottish place name and surname, also commonly used as a first name.
Famous names: Errol Flynn, actor; Errol Garner, jazz pianist.

Erskine [er-skin]
Meaning: possibly 'green ascent'.
   A surname, derived from a place name in Renfrewshire, this is now used as a first name.
Famous name: Erskine Childers, author

Eudard. *See* EDWARD

Euan. *See* EWAN

Evan. *See* EWAN

Evander [ev-an-der]
Meaning: from 'good man' in Greek.
In classical legend Evander is the name of an Arcadian hero who founded a city in Italy where Rome was later built. In Scotland, it has become a Highland name used as the anglicized form of the Gaelic Iomhar. In this form it is peculiar to the MacIver family, 'Son of Iomhar'.

Everard. *See* EWART

Ewan [yoo-an]
Meaning: 'young warrior' in Celtic.
Popularly associated with HUGH because of the similar pronunciation.
Variant spellings: Euan, Ewen

Gaelic cognate: Eoghann
Famous name: Ewan McCol, folksinger; Ewan MacGregor, actor.

Ewart [yoo-art]
Meaning: 'with the strength of a boar'.
This is the Scottish form of the English name Everard. It was introduced to England by the Normans.

Ewing [yoo-ing]
A Scottish name meaning 'fiery'.

Farquhar[far-kwar]
Meaning: 'manly' or 'very dear one' in Celtic.
The name is derived from Fearchur Fada, a seventh-century king of Dalriada, some time after St Columba's death.

There is a Cill Fhearchair ('Fearchar's cell' of 'Fearchar's church') in Kintail, suggesting that there was a bearer of the name in the Celtic Church.

The name has also resulted in the surname Farquarson.
Gaelic cognate: Fearchar

Fearchar. *See* FARQUAR

Fearghas. *See* FERGUS

Fergus [fer-ghus]
Meaning: 'man of virtue', 'manly strength' or 'supreme choice' in Celtic.
It is thought by some that Fearghus I (in 330 BC) was at the head of a line of Scottish kings about the same time as Alexander the Great, 600 years or so before the first Scottish settlers from Ireland arrived in Galloway and Argyll.

In the sixth century, Fearghus, a Dalriad prince, was blessed by St Patrick and led a great migration of Scots to Argyll with his brothers, Loarn and Aonnghus (ANGUS).

St Ferghas was apparently an eighth-century Pict who returned from Ireland as a bishop and travelled throughout northern Scotland.
Variant spelling: Feargus
Diminutive: Fergie
Gaelic cognate: Fearghas
Famous name: Fergus Keelie, radio presenter.

Fife [fyfe]
Meaning: possibly 'path'.
This Scottish shire name is also a surname, and is sometimes used as a first name.

Filip. *See* PHILIP

Findlay. *See* FINLAY

Fingal [fing-ul]
Meaning: from 'white stranger' in Gaelic.
FIONN mac Cumhail, known in Scotland as Fingal, was the greatest hero of the Scottish Gaelic tales. King Cormac appointed him chief of the Fianna, or Fenians, of whose heroic and romantic deeds there are many tales. He was chosen for his wisdom and generosity.

St Fionan was revered as a saint of great power and is commemorated in place names throughout Scotland.

An historical Fionnghal was the king of Man and Islec in the eleventh century.
Gaelic cognates: Fionn, Fionngal, Fionan

Finlay [fin-lee]
Meaning: from the Gaelic for 'fair warrior'.
Finlay was the father of Macbeth, king of Scotland. It was originally a surname, but is now also used as a first name.
Variant spelling: Findlay
Gaelic cognate: Fionnlagh
Famous name: Finlay Macdonald, author.

Finnean [fin-nyan]
Meaning: 'white' and 'head' in Gaelic.

Fionan. *See* FINGAL

Fionn [fyoon]
Meaning: 'white' or 'fair' in Gaelic.
Fionn mac Cumhail, also known as FINGAL, was the greatest
hero of the Scottish Gaelic tales.

Fionnlagh. *See* FINLAY

Fleming [flem-ming]
Meaning: 'refugee'.

Forbes [forbs]
Meaning: 'prosperous field' or 'prosperous district' in Gaelic.
This Aberdeen place name was a surname before being used
as a first name.
    Legend has it that the Forbes clan descended from
Ochonocar. He killed a boar which terrorized anyone who
tried to live in Donside, the braes of Forbes. After he had
dealt with the boar his family settled there.

Fordyce [for-dice]
Meaning: a Scottish name meaning 'man of wisdom'.

Francis [fran-sis]
Meaning: 'Frenchman'.
The widespread use of this name is undoubtedly due to St
Francis of Assisi. Born the son of a wealthy cloth merchant
of Assisi, he renounced his inheritance and founded the
Franciscan Order. Living in extreme and deliberate poverty
he rebuilt the small church of San Damiano with money
begged from the townsmen. He travelled as a pilgrim and
tended the lepers, but his legend always associates him with

animals and his ability to tame them.
Diminutive: Frank
Gaelic cognate: Frang
Famous names: Francis Bacon, Elizabethan philosopher; Frank Bruno, boxer.

Frang. *See* FRANCIS

Frank. *See* FRANCIS

Fraser [fray-zer]
Meaning: 'strawberries'.
A family of Norman origin took their name from that of the strawberry plant, *fraise*, the flower of which is used in their coat of arms.

A Norman knight named Frizel brought the name to Scotland, where it was first used only as a surname before also becoming a first name.
Variant spelling: Frazer
Gaelic cognate: Friseal

Friseal. *See* FRASER

Fulton [ful-tin]
This first name is the transferred use of the surname, which was originally a local place name in Ayrshire.

Gaban. *See* GAVIN

Gavin [ga-vin]
Meaning: 'white hawk' in Celtic, or derived from 'district of land' in Old German.
In Arthurian legend Gawain was a Knight of the Round Table and nephew of King Arthur. Gawain was a popular name in the Middle Ages. Gavin was a name particularly used by the Dunbars.
   Gavin Dunbar was archbishop of Glasgow and Lord Chancellor of Scotland in James V's reign. Gavin, bishop of Dunkeld, translated Virgil into Scots.
Variant spellings: Gavan, Gaven, Gavyn, Gawain, Guy
Gaelic cognate: Gabhan
Famous names: Gavin Maxwell, author; Gavin Hastings, rugby player.

Geordie. *See* GEORGE

George [jorj]
Meaning: derived from the Greek for 'earthworker' or 'husbandman'.
St George was a Roman military tribune martyred at Nicodemia in 306. (The dragon-killing legends were attached to his name later.) He was deeply revered in the East and the Emperor Constantine had a church erected in his honour. His cult was brought to England from the East by the Crusaders. Edward III founded the Order of the Garter on St George's Day in 1349, and from then he was regarded as the patron saint of England.
Variant spelling: Geordie
Gaelic cognate: Seoras
Famous names: George Mackay Brown, poet and novelist;

George Gershwin, composer; George Orwell, author; George Stephenson, railway engineer.

Gilbert [gil-burt]
Meaning: derived from two words in Old German meaning 'bright pledge'.
The name was brought to Britain by the Normans and became common in Scotland from an early date by virtue of its being used as the equivalent of the Gaelic Gilbride, 'servant of St Bridget'.

Gilleabart was the name of a twelfth-century king of Galloway and of the saint from Moray who became bishop of Caithness and founded Dornoch Cathedral. He founded the only religious order in England for both men and women. The Gilbertine order was suppressed by Henry VIII and all its houses appropriated.
Gaelic cognate: Gilleabart
Famous names: Gilbert White, author; Gilbert Chesterton, author.

Gilbride. *See* GILBERT

Gilchrist [gil-krist]
Meaning: from the Celtic for 'a servant of Christ'.
In 1267, Alexander III bestowed on the MacNaughtons' chief, Gilchrist, the island in Loch Awe on which the ruins of their castle can still be seen.
Gaelic cognate: Gillechriosd

Gildroy. *See* GILROY

Giles [jiles]
Meaning: from 'kid' in Greek.

The significance of this name lies in the early use of kid leather for shields.

St Giles is said to be a sixth-century Athenian who fled to France to escape the veneration his miracles aroused. A legend tells about his protection of a pet deer wounded in a hunt by the Visigoth king Wamba. The king found the deer, he had shot with an arrow, in the arms of St Giles. He is the patron saint of beggars and cripples. A number of churches are dedicated to him, including the High Kirk in Edinburgh.

This name is both a masculine and a feminine one.

Famous name: Giles Brandreth, journalist.

Gilleabart. *See* GILBERT

Gillean [gil-eean]
Meaning: from 'servant of St John' in Gaelic.
As a first name it is especially popular in the Clan Maclean, and it also occurs as a surname.
Variant spellings: Gilleon, Gillian
Gaelic cognate: Gilleathain

Gilleasbaig. *See* ARCHIBALD

Gilleathain. *See* GILLEAN

Gillechriosd. *See* GILCHRIST

Gillespie. *See* ARCHIBALD

Gilmour [gil-mor]
Meaning: 'servant of Mary' in Celtic.
The Morrison clan took their name from a Chief Maurice, after being known earlier as MacGilmore.

Gilmour is now used as a first name as well as a surname.
Variant spelling: Gilmore

Gilroy [gil-roy]
Meaning: from 'servant of the red-haired man' in Gaelic.
Variant spelling: Gildroy

Glen [glen]
Meaning: from the Gaelic for 'narrow mountain valley'.
A place name which became a surname, it began to be used as a first name in the early nineteenth century.
Variant spelling: Glenn
Famous names: Glen Hoddle, footballer; Glenn Miller, musician.

Gordon [gor-don]
Meaning: 'three-cornered hill' in Scots.
This place name became famous as a clan name. The Gordons, however, are of greater interest as a family than a tribal clan. In one story, the first of the family rescue a Scottish king from a wild boar. Although all-powerful in the north in medieval times, it was as landowners rather than patriarchal chiefs that the Gordons flourished. The modern use of it as a first name is due to the popularity of General Gordon of Khartoum.
Variant spellings: Gordan, Gorden
Famous names: Gordon Inglis, television presenter; Gordon Brown, Chancellor of the Exchequer.

Graham [gray-ham]
Meaning: from 'gravelly place' or 'homestead' in Old English.
A place name, clan name and surname, now used as a first

name. It was introduced into Scotland by the Norman William de Graham in the early twelfth century. He was given the lands of Abercorn and Dalkeith by David I and was present at the erection of the great Abbey of Holyrood and witnessed its charter.

Graham of Claverhouse, first Viscount Dundee, was a royalist officer who executed the severities of government in Scotland during the reigns of Charles II and James II. He was killed at the battle of Killiecrank.

Variant spellings: Grahame, Graeme (used almost exclusively in Scotland).

Gaelic cognate: Greum

Famous names: Graham Gooch, cricketer; Graeme Souness, footballer; Graham Greene, author.

Grant [grant]

Meaning: derived from a Norman nickname meaning 'large'. It was originally a surname. The Grants were a clan who gained a foothold in the Highlands through marriage settlement or other legal means, then extended their possessions by the sword. They were supporters of Robert the Bruce, and his victory confirmed the Grants in their holdings in Strathspey and firmly established them as Highland chiefs.

Greg [greg]

Meaning: 'fierce' in Celtic.

This is a name in its own right.

Variant spellings: Gregg, Greig.

Gregor [greg-or]

Meaning: from 'watchful' in Greek.

This is the Scottish form of Gregory. It became a popular

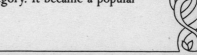

first name because of the fame of St Gregory (c. 540–604) and the fact that 'watchman' was a very appropriate term for a shepherd of the church. Gregory the Great was one of the greatest of the early popes, a reformer of monastic discipline and a prolific author. He is supposed to have sent Augustine to England. He gave his name to Gregorian Chant.

Many surnames ranging from Greer to Macgregor testify to its frequent use in Scotland in the Middle Ages. Originally MacGregor, the government outlawed the clan after a defeat at Glen Fruin in 1603, and the ban on using their surname was not lifted until 1784. The name Gregory was assumed by some members of the clan, among many 'Sept' names adopted by scattered groups of MacGregors.
Gaelic cognate: Griogair
Famous names: Gregor Fisher, comedian; Gregory Peck, actor; Gregor Mendel, scientist.

Gregory. *See* GREGOR

Greig [graeg]
Meaning: 'sun' or 'throne' in Persian.
This is the name of an infant martyr in Tarsus who is commemorated in the place name Eaglais Ghreig, in Kincardineshire.

A Greig, son of Donald I, was Gregory the Great, known as the Liberator of the Scottish Church.
Cognate: Cyrus.

Guy. *See* GAVIN

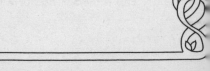

Halbert [hal-bert]
Meaning: 'bright stone' in Old German, and derivatively 'stone hard'.
This surname is also used as a first name, and is sometimes thought to be derived from the halberd, a long-shafted axe-like weapon.

Hamilton [ham-il-ton]
Meaning: possibly derived from a place name meaning 'scarred hill'.
Sir William de Hambleton fled from the court of Edward II to Scotland. He and his attendant changed clothes with two woodcutters to avoid their pursuers, and were using their saws in the act of cutting through an oak tree when their pursuers passed by. Sir William cried 'through'. If heard, this could have meant cutting through the tree, but in fact it meant that their pursuers were passing through. After his marriage to the daughter of the Earl of Strathern, he took for his crest an oak tree with a saw through it, and for his motto, 'Through'.
  Hamilton is now also used as a first name.
Famous name: Hamilton Harty, conductor.

Hamish. *See* JAMES

Hector [hek-tor]
Meaning: 'defender' in Greek; 'horseman' in Gaelic.
In Greek mythology, Hector was a Trojan hero in the Trojan War. Slain by Achilles, his body was lashed to Achilles' chariot and dragged round Troy three times.
  Achaius, king of Scotland, was supposed to have married a sister of the King of the Picts. An ally of Charlemagne, he formed an alliance against the Anglo-Saxons. While

marching his troops against the English forces, the cross of St Andrew was said to have appeared above them in the sky, giving an assurance of victory. It was adopted as the ensign of the Picts and afterwards of the Scots.

The Gaelic name Achaius became Eachann in the Highlands, and was then converted to Hector.

Gaelic cognate: Eachann

Famous names: Hector Munro, author who wrote under the pseudonym 'Saki'.

Hilary [hil-a-ree]
Meaning: from the Latin *hilarius*, meaning 'cheerful'.

The bishop St Hilarius of Poitiers (d. 368) was a champion of the Church against Arian heresy. His feast day, 13 January, gives the Hilary Term, one of the four portions of the year in which the High Court sits, its name.

Initially a boy's name, Hilary is now also a girl's name.

Variant spellings: Hillary, Hillery.

Gaelic cognate: Falair

Hugh [hew]
Meaning: from a Germanic word meaning 'heart' or 'mind'.

Little Hugh of Lincoln was a child supposed in the Middle Ages to have been murdered by a Jew named Copin or Joppin at Lincoln. The body is said to have been discovered in a well, buried near the Cathedral, and to have been the cause of several miracles. The story is referred to by Chaucer in *The Prioress's Tale*.

Because of similarities in pronunciation, Hugh is used in Scotland as the equivalent of several Gaelic names such as Uisdean, Eoghann and Aodh.

Famous names: Hugh Grant, actor; Sir Hugh Walpole, author; Hugh Laurie, comedian.

Huntly [hunt-lee]
Meaning: 'hunting ley' or 'meadow'.
Originally a place name and surname, now sometimes used
as a first name. A sept of the Gordon clan, the Huntleys had
their origin in the Berwickshire lands of Gordon.

Ian [ee-un]
Meaning: from the Hebrew for 'God is gracious'.
It is the Scottish Gaelic form of John. As the name of two saints, St John the Baptist and St John the Evangelist, it became a popular Christian name.

This name's chief use was originally in the Eastern Church and it only became common in the West after the first Crusades.
Gaelic cognate: Iain
Famous names: Ian Cuthbertson, actor; Ian McCaskill, television weather presenter; Ian Fleming, author; Iain Burnside, radio presenter.

Innes [in-is]
Meaning: from the Gaelic *innes*, meaning 'islet'.
The island in question was one near Elgin on land granted to the Innes' ancestor, Berowald, in 1154 by Malcolm IV for service against rebelling Moray tribes.

Innes became a surname then later a clan name. As a first name, it is usually used as boy's name, but can also be a girl's name.
Variant spelling: Innis; sometimes thought to be a variation of Angus.

Iomhar. *See* EVANDER

Iorcall [yor-cull) or (eer-cull]
Cognate with Hercules, derived from the Greek Heracles, mythical hero of strength.

Irvine [er-vin]
Meaning: 'west river' (Iar Avon).
It was first a surname deriving from a place name – the

town of Irvine on the river Irvine. Now it is used as a first name too.

The Irvingites were a religious body founded about 1835 from a revivalist circle that was partly inspired by the teachings of Edward Irving (1792–1834), a Scottish minister. They believed that the second coming of Christ was near and wanted the re-establishment of the old offices of the Church (prophets, apostles, evangelists, and so on).

Variant spellings: Irwin, Irving
Famous name: Irving Berlin, composer.

Ivor [eye-vu]

Meaning: composed of the elements 'bow' and 'army' in Old Norse, possibly meaning 'archer'.

It gave rise to such Scottish surnames as MacIvor, and MacIver.

Variant spelling: Iver
Famous names: Ivor Novello, composer; Ivor Gurney, poet.

Ivy [eye-vee]

A plant name used as a first name from the 1860s. In Scotland it is found regularly as a boy's name – a pet form of IVOR.

James [jaems]

Meaning: English form of Jacob, meaning 'supplanter'.

The apostle, St James the Great, son of Zebedee, was one of the most popular saints of the Middle Ages. He was the first apostle to die for the Christian faith.

According to legend, his relics were brought to Compostela, in Spain, and this became a pilgrimage centre.

In Scotland the name has strong royal associations. There were seven kings of that name, and James VI of Scotland became James I of England.

Hamish is the Scottish form of James.

Variant spellings: Jim, Jimmie, Jimmy
Gaelic cognate: Seumas
Famous names: James Barrie, author; Jim Davidson, comedian; James Cameron, journalist; James Naughtie, radio and television presenter; Jimmy Tarbuck, comedian and television personality.

Jamie [jae-mee]

Meaning: 'supplanter'.

In Scotland, this diminutive of JAMES is used as an independent name.

John. *See* IAN

Joseph [jo-zef]

Meaning: 'Jehovah adds' or 'Jehovah increases' in Hebrew.

The meaning of the name may relate to large families: Joseph was the twelfth son of Jacob. Like many biblical names it was used in Scotland and was popular until recent times.

Joseph, husband of the Virgin Mary, was one of many biblical figures of this name.

Gaelic cognate: Eosaph
Famous names: Joseph Brady, actor; Joseph Lister surgeon;
Joseph Conrad, author.

Joyce [joy-is]
Meaning: from *jocosa*, 'merry' in Latin.
This was originally a Celtic name. It was also borne by a
seventh-century Breton hermit, St Judoc, son of Juthael,
king of Brittany. It was said that after his death his body did
not decompose and his followers would periodically trim his
hair and beard.

Keeldar [keel-dar]
Meaning: derived from 'battle army' in Old German.

Keir [k-eer]
Meaning: derived from a Gaelic name meaning 'swarthy' or 'dusky'.
A surname, sometimes also used as a first name.
Famous name: James Keir Hardy, politician.

Keith [keeth]
Meaning: 'wind' or 'wood' in Gaelic.
Originally the surname of the earls of Kintore, whose family seat was at Keith Hall. Either they called their house by their surname, or took their name from their house.

The Keiths enjoyed the office of Marischal (or Keeper) of the Royal Mares long before one of their number distinguished themselves at Bannockburn. Afterwards they flourished as Scotland's Earls Marischals, founding a college at Aberdeen.
Gaelic cognate: Ce
Famous name: Keith Floyd, cookery writer and television chef; Keith Carradine, actor.

Kelvin [kel-vin]
Meaning: 'one who lives by a narrow stream'.
Originally the Celtic name of a Scottish river, it is now sometimes used as a first name.
Famous name: Kelvin MacKenzie, newspaper editor.

Kenneth [ken-neth]
Meaning: from 'fiery' or 'handsome' in Gaelic.
A canonized abbot, usually known as Canice or Canicus, bore the name Kenneth and preached in Scotland and

Ireland in the sixth century.

The name has been popular from the time of Kenneth MacAlpin (Winneach mac Ailpein), the first king of Scotland.

Diminutives: Ken, Kenny

Gaelic associate: Coinneach is popularly associated with Kenneth and is sometimes used as its equivalent. It is in fact derived from the Celtic *cannicos*, meaning 'fair one'.

Famous names: Kenneth MacKellar, singer; Kenneth Graham, author; Ken Loach, film director; Kenny Everett, radio presenter and comedian.

Kerr [kar]

Meaning: derived from a place name meaning 'brushwood', or from the Gaelic for 'spear'.

The Scottish Kerrs are recorded after Norman Conquest. Their main territory was Roxburghshire, where they were early sheriffs.

This famous Scottish surname, which often occurs in the history of Border warfare, is also used as a first name in Scotland.

Variant spellings: Car, Ker

Kevan [ke-vin]

Meaning: 'comely' or 'beloved' in Gaelic.

A variant of the English name Kevin. In Scotland it is both a surname and a first name.

Famous name: Kevin Keegan, footballer; Kevin Costner, actor.

Kirk [kerk]

Meaning: from 'church' in Old Norse.

This place name and surname is now also used as a first

name.

It originated in Perth in the fifteenth century.

Famous name: Kirk Douglas, actor and film director.

Kit. *See* CHRISTOPHER

Kyle [k-eye-l]

Meaning: from 'channel between islands' or 'handsome' in Gaelic.

The Kyles of Bute, very narrow straits between the Scottish coast and the island of Bute, are noted for their natural beauty.

This place name and surname is now also a first name, for both boys and girls.

Famous name: Kyle McLachlan, actor.

Labhrainn. *See* LAWRENCE

Lachlan [loch-lan]
Meaning: possibly derived from the Gaelic word 'Lochlann', meaning 'land of the lochs', or from the Old Norse for 'Norway' or 'fjord land'.

The name is preserved in the clan name Maclachlan, whose ancient clan home was Strathlachlan. According to tradition, the Maclachlans were related to the ancient kings of Ireland and Somerled Lords of the Isles.
Variant spelling: Lachie
Gaelic cognate: Lachlann

Latharn. *See* LORNE

Laurie. *See* LAWRENCE

Lawrence [lor-ens]
Meaning: 'from the town of Laurentum' in Latin. The place name may be derived from *laurus*, the laurel or bay tree.

St Laurence the Deacon, martyred in Rome in 258 by being roasted on a grid-iron, is the patron saint of curriers.
Variant spellings: Laurence; Laurie, a pet name sometimes used as a name in its own right.
Gaelic cognate: Labhrainn
Famous names: Sir Laurence Olivier, actor; Laurie Taylor, radio presenter; Lawrence Sterne, author.

Lennox [len-ox]
Meaning: possibly connected with 'elm'.
This Scottish place name is sometimes used as a first name both for boys and girls.
Famous name: Sir Lennox Berkeley, composer.

Leslie [lez-lee]
Meaning: possibly from 'low-lying meadow' or 'garden by a pond' in Gaelic.
A Scottish place name and a well-known Scottish surname, the family taking their name from Garrioch, the lands of Leslie in Aberdeenshire. It is also the surname of the Earls of Rothes, in Moray.

Leslie has been used as a first name for both boys and girls since the end of the nineteenth century.
Feminine form: LESLEY
Famous names: Leslie Charteris, author; Leslie Crowther, television personality.

Lewis [loo-is]
Meaning: 'low island' or 'marsh'.
Originally Lewis was a form of the French name Louis and German name Ludwig. It is now regarded as a name in its own right.
Gaelic cognate: Luthais
Famous names: Lewis Carroll, author; Lewis Grassic Gibbon, author.

Lindsay [lind-see]
Meaning: possibly 'of gentle speech' in Old German.
The name of a famous Scottish family and the surname of the Earls of Crawford.
Variant spellings: LINDSEY (usually feminine), Linsey, Lyndsey.

Lodowick [lod-o-wik]
Meaning: 'devoted to the Lord'.
This is the Scottish form of Ludovic. Maoldomhnaich, is the Gaelic form, meaning 'tonsured servant' (*maol*) 'of Sunday.' (*Domhnaich*).

It was a name given to boys supported by the Sunday collection in church.
Variant spelling: Ludo
Gaelic cognate: Maoldomhnaich
Famous name: Ludovic Kennedy, journalist and author.

Logan [lo-gun]
Meaning: 'small hollow' in Gaelic.
A Scottish place name and surname, also used as a first name.

Lorne [lorn]
Meaning: derived from the Celtic word *lovernos* (fox).
The place name Lorn, in Argyllshire, gave rise to this name, which can be used for both boys and girls.

Latharn was the founder of Cineal Lethairn, one of the three main regions of the early Scottish kingdom of Dalriada.

The Appin clan are descendants of the last Lord Lorne, who died in 1469.
Feminine form: LORN
Gaelic cognate: Latharn

Ludovic. *See* LODOWICK

Luthais. *See* LEWIS

Lyle [l-eye-l]
Meaning: derived from 'someone who came from the island' in Anglo-Norman. It is used as both a first name and a surname.
Annot Lyle is a character in Scott's novel, *A Legend of Montrose*, the story of the campaign of 1644, when the

Highland clans inflicted a series of defeats on their opponents, the Scottish covenanters.

Famous name: Lyle Lovatt, country and western singer.

Lyndsey. *See* LINDSAY

Lyulf [leye-ulf]
Meaning: 'fire' and 'wolf' in Old English.
Variant spelling: Lyulph

Macauley. *See* AULEY

Macdonald [mac-don-ald]
Meaning: 'son of Donald'.
The largest and most widespread clan, the Clan Donald has its main roots in the old Gaelic and Pictish times.

The first clear ancestor is Somerled, thane of Argyll, who was almost an independent king of the South Isles.

This famous clan name and surname is quite often used as a Scottish first name.
Famous name: George MacDonald Fraser, novelist.

Magnus [mag-nus]
Meaning: 'great' in Latin.
This name, which reached Scotland via Shetland, became Manas in Gaelic. St Manas founded Kirkwall Cathedral, in Orkney. He was murdered by his cousin and co-earl of Orkney and is buried in Kirkwall Cathedral.

The first person to bear the name was Magnus I, king of Norway and Denmark, who died in 1047. His father was a great admirer of Charlemagne (Carolus Magnus). The story is told that the child, Magnus, was baptized by his father's servants, who thought that Magnus was a personal name.
Gaelic cognate: Manas
Famous name: Magnus Magnusson, television presenter and author.

Malcolm [mal-com]
Meaning: 'servant of Columba' in Celtic.
This name is derived from that of Columba, the sixth-century saint who founded the religious settlement of Iona.

There have been four Scottish kings with the name Malcolm, including Malcom III, son of Duncan, the king

murdered by Macbeth.
Gaelic cognate: CALUM
Famous names: Sir Malcolm Sargent, conductor; Sir Malcolm Campbell, land speed record holder; Malcolm Bradbury, novelist; Malcolm Muggeridge, journalist, author and television presenter.

Malise [mal-ees]
Meaning: 'servant of Jesus' in Gaelic.
A former favourite name with the GRAHAMS and borne by several earls of Strathearn. It survives as a surname in the form of Mellis.
Gaelic cognate: Maoilios

Manas. *See* MAGNUS

Maoldomhnaich. *See* LODOWICK

Maoilios. *See* MALISE

Marshall [mar-shall]
Meaning: 'horse servant' in Old German.
As a surname, Marshall may indicate either an ancestor who was a farrier, or one who was an officer in the royal household responsible for important ceremonies.
    It is regularly used as a first name.
Famous name: Marshall McLuhan, author.

Martin [mar-tin]
Meaning: in Latin the name is connected with Mars, god of war, so possibly means 'belonging to Mars' or 'war-like'.
St Martin of Tours, a fourth-century soldier, later bishop of Tours, was the founder of monasticism in Gaul. He became

a Christian at an early age, but was conscripted into the Roman army. After protesting (perhaps an early example of conscientious objection) he was imprisoned.

After the hostilities were over, it was at Amiens that St Martin cut his cloak in half to clothe a nearly naked beggar. This episode was followed by a dream in which Christ was wearing the cloak he had given away. He then became a disciple of Hilary at Poitiers and was baptized. He performed good works and worked miracles, and became the patron saint of tavern keepers.

Martin and MacMartin are common Scottish surnames.

Variant spelling: Martyn
Gaelic cognate: Martainn
Famous names: Martyn Lewis, television news presenter; Martin Luther, religious reformer; Martin Amis, novelist.

Mata. *See* MATTHEW

Matthew [math-eew]
Meaning: 'Gift of God' in Hebrew.
In the New Testament, St Matthew was a tax collector until he was called to be an apostle. He also wrote the first Gospel.

Introduced by the Normans, the name has long been popular in Scotland.

Variant spelling: Matthias
Diminutives: Matt, Mat (the pet form).
Gaelic cognate: Mata
Famous names: Matthew Arnold, poet; Matthew Kelly, television personality.

Maxwell [max-well]
Meaning: derived from 'greatest' or 'biggest' in Latin, or

from a place name, Maccus' well, a fishing-reach of the River Tweed near Kelso.

Originally a surname, it is now used also as a first name. When used as a first name it is usually abbreviated to Max.

Maxwells could have been established in Scotland since the tenth century, deriving from Maccus, a tenth century king of Man and the Isles, but it is more likely that they were descended from a Norman family, settled there by MALCOLM Canmore and destined to hold high office thereafter.

Famous names: Max Beerbolm, critic and caricaturist; Max Bygraves, singer and comedian.

Melville [mel-vil]

Meaning: 'bad settlement'.

This Norman place name became a Scottish surname and first name.

Variant spelling: Melvin, Melvyn

Diminutive: Mel

Famous names: Melvyn Bragg, author and television presenter; Herman Melville, author; Mel Gibson, actor.

Melvyn. *See* MELVILLE

Menzies [meng-iz]

Meaning: from the Latin for 'the merciful'.

This is a Scottish shortening of the name Clemence. The name came from one of the many Norman families that moved to Scotland around the twelfth century.

It was a Menzies who introduced the 'monkey puzzle' tree and the larch to Scotland about two centuries ago.

Famous name: Menzies Campbell, politician.

Michael [meye-kil]
Meaning: from the Hebrew, meaning 'who is like God?'
St Michael, patron saint of soldiers, is known throughout western Scotland as the patron of all things and people connected with seafaring, and of horses and horsemen. His feast day is 29 September (Michaelmas).

This name has been popular in Scotland from early times. Sir Michael Scott was a famous thirteenth-century scholar. He studied at Oxford, Bologna and Paris, and was attached to the court of Frederick II at Palermo as the official astrologer. Legends of his magical power were inspirational for many writers.
Gaelic cognate: Micheal
Diminutives: Mike, Mickey, Mitch
Famous names: Michael Heseltine, politician; Michael Aspel, television presenter; Mike Tyson, boxer; Mick Jagger, musician; Mickey de Lane, singer.

Micheal. *See* MICHAEL

Monro. *See* MUNRO

Moray. *See* MURRAY

Muir [meew-ir]
Meaning: 'dweller by the moor' in Scots.
Mainly a surname, it is also used as a first name.

Muireach. *See* MURDO

Mungo [mung-go]
Meaning: 'most dear' or 'amiable' in Celtic.
This was the nickname of St Kentigern, founder of Glasgow

Cathedral. It was his custom to sing the entire Book of Psalms every night standing up to his neck in water; for this he acquired the epithet 'Munghu the amiable'.
Gaelic cognate: Mungan
Famous name: Mungo Park, explorer; Mungo Jerry, musician.

Munro [mun-ro]
The origin of this name is much disputed. According to one theory, this Scottish surname, and subsequent first name, was brought to Scotland by people living in Ireland, near the River Roe, in County Derry – 'mouth of the Roe'.

Another theory refers the name to Ross, as the family were formerly vassals of the Earl of Ross.
Variant spelling: Monro

Murchadh. *See* MURDO

Murchison [mur-tch-i-son]
Meaning: a derivative of 'Mary's son'.

Murdo [mur-do]
Meaning: derived from one or other of the Gaelic names *Muireach* (mariner) or *Murchadh* (sea warrior).
Originally a surname, this is now also used as a first name.
Variant spellings: Murdoch, Murtoch
Gaelic cognate: Muireach, Murchadh

Murray [mu-ree]
Meaning: 'settlement beside the sea' in Celtic.
Now used as a first name, this surname is derived from the Scottish place name Moray. It is the surname of the Dukes of Atholl, the only family in Britain permitted to keep a private army.

In 1845, Queen Victoria presented a pair of colours to the Athole Highlanders, placing them in a unique position as the only private bodyguard in the country.

Variant spelling: Moray
Gaelic cognate: Moireach
Famous name: John Murray, Publishers; Murray Parahia, pianist.

Murtoch. *See* MURDO

Nanty. *See* ANTHONY

Neil [nee-ull]
Meaning: 'champion' in Celtic.
This is the Scottish form of Neal.

The legend of the name begins in the East, but it is not clear. It is said that Phenius taught a people the alphabet and left them his name, the Phoenicians. His son, Niul, married the pharoah's daughter and while on embassy in Egypt, named the Nile. A subsequent dispute with the Egyptians caused Niul's son (married to Scota) to migrate to Spain, whence his followers were called Scots.
Variant spellings: Niel, Neal, Neill
Gaelic cognate: Niall
Famous names: Neil Armstrong, astronaut; Neil Kinnock, politician; Neil Morrisey, actor.

Niall. *See* NEIL and NIGEL

Nicholas [nihk-o-las]
Meaning: a Greek name composed of elements meaning 'people's victory'.

Nicholas, reputed 4th-century bishop of Myra in Asia Minor, is the patron saint of Russia, and of children, scholars, sailors, virgins and thieves. His chief claim to fame is as the original Father Christmas, Santa Claus, taken from the Dutch *Sinte Claus*.

Nicol (the early spelling of the name) led to Scottish surnames such as MacNicol. The spelling Nicholas appeared in the Middle Ages.
Variant spellings: Nicolas, Nickolas
Diminutives: Nick, Nicki
Gaelic cognate: Niocal

Famous names: Nicholas Parsons, television personality; Nick Faldo, golfer; Nicholas Monsarrat, author.

Nicol. *See* NICHOLAS

Nigel [neye-jul]
Meaning: 'black' in Latin.
This form was adopted in addition to the Old Gaelic, Nial, through the inclusion of the numerous Anglo-Norman nobles in the Scottish peerage.

It is considered as peculiarly Scottish, and it occurs in the Domesday Book and in even earlier documents as a Scottish name.
Gaelic cognate: Niall
Famous names: Nigel Mansell, racing driver; Nigel Hawthorne, actor; Nigel Dempster, journalist; Nigel Lawson, politician.

Ninean. *See* NINIAN

Ninian[nin-ee-yun]j
This is a Scottish name of unknown Celtic origin.

Bishop Ninian, the first known missionary saint to Scotland, the Apostle of Cumberland and of the southern Picts of Scotland (the Benedictines), was a Brythonic Celt who received instruction in Rome, converted southern Scotland and built a church at Withorn. He exercised considerable influence amongst the Celts before he died in 432.
Gaelic cognate: Ninean

Niocal. *See* NICHOLAS

Norman [nor-man]
Meaning: a 'north man' or 'Norman'.
In the thirteenth century, the name Norman was carried to Scotland by English nobles.
Gaelic cognate: Tormod
Famous names: Norman Wisdom, comedian; Norman Tebbitt, politician; Norman Hartnell, fashion designer.

Odo [o-doh]
Meaning:' rich' in Old English.
It was the Scottish equivalent of the Gaelic name Aodh.

Olaf. *See* AULAY

Oliver. *See* AULAY

Paddy. *See* PATRICK

Padraig. *See* PATRICK

Parlan [par-lan]
Meaning: possibly 'waves of the sea'.
It is the origin of surnames such as Macfarlane and Macfarland, and is occasionally used as a first name.

Patrick [pat-rikh]
Meaning: 'noble man' in Latin.
St Patrick is thought to have been born in Dumbarton but as a boy was captured by pirates and sent to Ireland. He managed to escape and returned to Scotland, but was called to go back to Ireland as an evangelist.

His conscience would not let him stay at home while the people in his land of captivity remained pagans. So he trained as a missionary in France, returned to Ireland to teach them the Christian faith, and spent the rest of his life there.

In the Middle Ages, *The Ballad of Sir Patrick Spens* told of a quest to Norway to bring back a princess to marry the king.
Diminutives: Peter (a diminutive of PATRICK in Scotland), Pat, Paddy
Feminine form: PATRICIA
Gaelic cognate: Padraig
Famous names: Patrick Moore, astronomer; Patrick Macnee, actor; Sir Patrick Geddes, sociologist, author and town-planner; Paddy Ashdown, politician; Patrick Swayze, actor.

Paul [paul]
Meaning: 'small' in Latin.
In the Bible, Saul of Tarsus was renamed Paul, after his

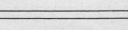

conversion to Christianity by a vision while on the road to Damascus. He wrote fourteen epistles, which form part of the New Testament.

The use of this name in Scotland in the Middle Ages led to such surnames as Polson, Macphail, Paulin and Paulson.

Gaelic cognate: Pol

Famous names: Paul Schofield, actor; Paul Gascoigne, footballer; Paul Newman, actor; Paul Keating, politician; Paul McKenna, magician and TV personality; Paul Theroux, author.

Peadar. *See* PETER

Peter [pee-ter]
Meaning: 'rock' in Greek.
St Peter was an apostle of Christ and the first pope. He wrote two epistles, which form part of the New Testament. According to tradition, he was martyred in Rome by being crucified upside down.

Peter is particularly popular in Scotland on account of its being the diminutive of PATRICK.

J.M. Barrie's *Peter Pan*, about a boy who would not grow up, also contributed to the popularity of the name.

Diminutive: Pete
Gaelic cognates: Padraig, Peadar
Famous names: Peter Sellers, actor; Peter Finch, actor; Peter Ustinov, actor; Pete Townsend, musician; Pete Sampras, tennis player; Peter Carey, author;

Philip [fil-lip]
Meaning: 'lover of horses' in Greek.
In earlier times in Fife, the local pronunciation of the name led to the surname Philp.
Variant spelling: Phillip
Gaelic cognate: Filip

Famous names: Prince Philip, consort of Queen Elizabeth II; Phil Collins, singer and songwriter; Philip Scofield, television personality.

Pol. *See* PAUL

Quinton [kwin-ton]
Meaning: 'fifth' in Latin.
Very little is known about the life of St Quentin of Amiens. He appears to have been a Roman citizen who came to preach the gospel in Gaul. He was arrested by the prefect, who finally killed him after a series of gruesome tortures, illustrated in the early medieval Life of the saint, which survives at St Quentin. He was revered in many English medieval monasteries and became patron saint of Kirkmahoe in Dumfriesshire. His feast day is 31 October.
Variant spelling: Quentin
Gaelic cognate: Caointean
Famous name: Quentin Crisp, author.

Rab. *See* ROBERT

Raghnall. *See* RONALD

Raibert. *See* ROBERT

Ralston [ral-ston]
Meaning: 'settlement' in Old Norse.
Since the thirteenth century a Scottish place name and surname, it is now also used as a first name.

Ramsay [rams-ee]
Meaning: possibly 'wild garlic island'.
A Scottish place name which became a surname and is now used as a first name.
    The Ramsays have been established in Midlothian since the twelfth century, and are now a clan in their own right.
Variant spelling: Ramsey
Famous names: James Ramsay MacDonald, politician; Ramsey Campbell, author.

Ranald. *See* RONALD

Randal. *See* RANDOLF

Randolf [ran-dolf]
Meaning: from the Old Norse for 'wolf shield'.
Variant spellings: Randal, Randall, Ranulph, Ranult
Famous names: Ranulph Fiennes, polar explorer and author; Randall Scott, actor.

Reginald. *See* RONALD

Reid [reed]
Meaning: 'red' or 'red-haired'.
It was a surname but is now also used as a first name.

Reynold. *See* RONALD

Richard [rich-ard]
Meaning: an Old German name derived from the elements for 'power', 'hardy', 'brave' or 'strong', meaning 'powerful ruler'.
Richard I the Lionheart led the Third Crusade in the twelfth century.
  Early use of this name in Scotland led to the surnames Dickinson, Dick, Dickson, Ritchie and Richieson.
Gaelic cognates: Ridseard, Ruiseart
Diminutives: Dick, Ricki, Rich, Ritchi, Richie
Famous names: Richard Wilson, actor; Dick Whittington, Lord Mayor of London; Rik Mayle, actor; Sir Richard Attenborough, actor.

Ridseard. *See* RICHARD

Ritchie. *See* RICHARD

Robaidh. *See* ROBERT

Roban. *See* ROBERT

Robert [rob-ert]
Meaning: 'fame' and 'bright' in Old German.
Borne by three kings of Scotland, it was also the name of Scotland's national hero, Robert the Bruce, who freed Scotland from English domination, and of the legendary

Scottish outlaw, Robert MacGregor (Rob Roy).
Gaelic cognates: Raibeart, Roban, Robaidh, Rab
Diminutives: Robin, Rabbie, Rob, Robbie, Bob, Bobby
Famous names: Robbie Coltrane, Robert Urquhart, actor; Robert Carlyle, actor; Robert Burns, poet; Sir Robert Peel, politician; Robert Graves, author; Robert de Niro, actor.

Robin. *See* ROBERT

Roderick [rod-er-ikh]
Meaning: made up of 'fame' and 'power' in Old German.
Roderick, who died in battle against the Saracens in AD 711 was the last Visigoth king of Spain. The name was taken up by the Scots and often occurs in the clan histories.
Variant spelling: Roderic
Diminutives: Derick (the Scottish short form which is used as a name in its own right), Rod, Roddy
Famous name: Roddy McDowell, actor.

Roidh. *See* ROY

Ronald [ron-ald]
Meaning: elements of Old Norse meaning 'power' and 'counsel'.
Raghnall was the name of a twelfth-century Earl of Orkney, a nephew of St MAGNUS, who founded Kirkwall Cathedral and was canonized. Ronald is the popular Scottish version of Reginald, now established as a name in its own right.
Variant spellings: Ranald, Reginald, Reynold
Diminutive: Ronny, Ronnie
Gaelic cognate: Raghnall
Famous names: Ronnie Barker and Ronnie Corbett, comedians; Ronald Reagan, statesman.

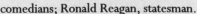

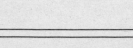

Rory [ror-ee]
Meaning: from the Gaelic for 'red'.
Gaelic cognate: Ruairidh
Famous name: Rory Bremner, comedian.

Ross [ross]
Meaning: 'promontory'.
A Scottish place name and surname, now also used as a first name. The ancient Celtic earldom of Ross in the north-west Highlands was established in the thirteenth century, and reverted to the Crown on the forfeiture of the lordship of the Isles in 1476.
Gaelic cognate: Ros

Roy [roy]
Meaning: from the Gaelic for 'red'.
Sir Walter Scott's *Rob Roy*, a novel about a real Scottish outlaw, ROBERT MacGregor, might have had some bearing on the name's popularity.
Gaelic cognate: Roidh
Famous names: Roy Marsden, actor; Roy Hattersley, politician; Roy Hudd, comedian; Roy Kinnear, comedian; Roy Orbison, singer.

Ruairidh. *See* RORY

Ruiseart. *See* RICHARD

Sandaidh. *See* ALASDAIR

Sandy. *See* ALASDAIR

Saunder. *See* ALASDAIR

Scott [skot]
Meaning: 'dart'.
This name is derived from the surname meaning 'Scot', and originated as a by-name for someone from Scotland.
Famous names: F. Scott Fitzgerald, author; Scott Simpson, golf champion.

Seoras. *See* GEORGE

Seumas. *See* JAMES

Sholto [shol-toe]
Meaning: possibly a derivation from the Gaelic word for 'sower'.
The name occurs in Scottish clan histories and is occasionally used as a first name.

Sim. *See* SIMON

Simeon. *See* SIMON

Simon [seye-mon]
Meaning: from 'snub-nosed' in Greek, or from 'hearing' in Hebrew.
The popularity of Simon as a first name in the Middle Ages was due to its association with Simon Peter, the apostle.
St Simon Stylites, the fifth-century Syrian saint, spent

thirty-six years on top of a pillar in prayer and fasting.

The pet forms Sim, Sime, Sym, Syme and Simmie gave rise to surnames such as Simpkins, Simpson and Simson but the name is historically associated with the Frasers.

The Chief of clan Fraser of Lovat is called MacShimi, son of Simon.

Variant spelling: Simeon
Gaelic cognate: Sim
Famous names: Simon Gray, playwright; Simon Callow, actor; Simon le Bon, pop star.

Sinclair [sin-clair]
Originally Saint-Clair, a name of unknown origin, but probably a Norman baronial name, which was transferred to Scotland as a surname in the twelfth century. It is now also used as a first name.
Famous name: Sinclair Lewis, novelist.

Solas [soh-lus]
Meaning: 'joy', 'comfort', 'solace' in Gaelic.

Steafen. *See* STEPHEN

Steaphen. *See* STEPHEN

Stephen [stee-ven]
Meaning: 'crown' or 'garland' in Greek.
St Stephen was the first Christian martyr. He was one of seven deacons appointed by the apostles to see to the distribution of alms to the faithful and to help in the Christian ministry. While preaching to the Jews he attacked his hearers for resisting the spirit and killing Christ. They stoned him for blasphemy. From early times he was the

patron of deacons and in the later Middle Ages he was invoked against headaches. He is patron of innumerable churches, and in England forty-six churches, built after the Norman Conquest, are dedicated to him.

Steen was the early pronunciation of Stephen in Fife and the Lothians, leading to surnames such as Stein and Staines.
Variant spellings: Steaphen, Steven (the more popular modern spelling).
Gaelic cognate: Steafan
Famous names: Stevie Wonder, singer and songwriter; Steven Spielberg, film director; Sir Stephen Spender, author; Stephen King, author; Steve Martin, comedian and actor; Stephen Sondheim, songwriter; Steve Biko, political activist.

Steven. *See* STEPHEN

Steward. *See* STUART

Stewart. *See* STUART

Stiubhart. *See* STUART

Struan [strue-un]
Meaning: possibly derived from 'little stream'.
The chiefs of clan Donachie (Robertson) formerly possessed the lands of Struan or Strowan, in Perthshire. Struan is sometimes used as a first name.

Stuart [stew-art]
Meaning: 'steward' or 'chief of the royal household'.
It was from Walter fitz Alan, the Norman noble appointed hereditary High Steward of Scotland by David I, that the Stewart kings descended. Mary, Queen of Scots used the

form Stuart and the House of Stuart ruled Scotland from 1371 and England from 1603 until 1714.

Variant spellings: Stewart, Steward
Gaelic cognate: Stiubhart
Famous name: Stuart Granger, actor.

Syme. *See* SIMON

Thane [thane]
Meaning: from 'servant' in Old English.
Thane is the title of a clan chief in Scotland. He held land given by the king and ranked equal with an earl's son. It has been used as a name since the nineteenth century.

Thomas [tom-as]
Meaning: 'twin' in Aramaic.
Thomas was one of the twelve apostles. Originally this was a nickname used to distinguish one of the three Judahs in the New Testament.

The name was made famous by the martyrdom of Thomas à Beckett, murdered in Canterbury Cathedral in 1170.

The cathedral became a centre of pilgrimage and the name Thomas became popular all over Britain, including Scotland.

The expression 'every Tom, Dick and Harry' shows how often Thomas was used as a first name.
Variant spellings: Tomas, Tammas
Diminutives: Tom, Tommy, Tam
Gaelic cognate: Tomas
Famous names: Tom Conti, actor; Thomas Carlyle, author and historian; Thomas Hardy, novelist; Tommy Steele, musician; Thomas Gainsborough, painter; Tom Cruise, actor.

Timothy [tim-o-thee]
Meaning: derived from 'honour God' in Greek.
This name is used both in Scotland and Ireland as a substitute for Tadhg, a local name meaning poet or philosopher.

In the New Testament, Timothy was converted by St Paul and became his companion. It is said that he was beaten to

death by a mob in AD 97 for opposing the worship of the goddess Diana.
Famous name: Timothy West, actor.

Tomas. *See* THOMAS

Tony. *See* ANTHONY

Tormod. *See* NORMAN

Torquil [tor-kil]
Meaning: from 'Thor's cauldron' in Old Norse.
This is a Scottish name from the Gaelic, Torcall, itself derived from a Norse name. A Torquil was the founder of the MacLeods of Lewis, in the Outer Hebrides, and the name is much used by the clan.

A character called Torquil appears in Sir Walter Scott's novel *Fair Maid of Perth*, set at the close of the fourteenth century when Robert III was king of Scotland.
Gaelic cognate: Torcall

Trent [trent]
Meaning: 'one who lives by a stream' in Celtic.
A place name and surname which is now used as a first name as well.

Uallas. *See* WALLACE

Uilleam. *See* WILLIAM

Uisdean. *See* HUGH

Vivian [viv-ee-en]
Meaning: derived from the Latin for 'alive'.
The name of an obscure Christian martyr of the fifth century.
Feminine form: VIVIEN.
Famous name: Viv Richards, cricketer.

Wallace [wal-lis]

Meaning: as a surname, 'stranger'.
William Wallace (1272–1305) was a Scottish patriot known as the scourge of England. He fought for Scottish independence but was betrayed to the English. He was hanged, drawn and quartered at Westminster Hall, in London.
Variant spelling: Wallis
Diminutives: Wal, Wally
Gaelic cognate: Uallas
Famous name: Wallace Stevens, poet.

Walter [wal-ter]

Meaning: from an Old German name, made up of the elements 'rule' and 'folk'.
The Border clan, the Scotts, used this name for generations, and the Scottish royal house of Stuart descended from a Walter.
Gaelic cognate: Bhaltair
Famous names: Sir Walter Scott, author; Sir Walter Raleigh, navigator and courtier.

Ward [ward]

Meaning: 'watchman' or 'guardian'.
This is a transferred use of an occupational and aristocratic surname. It is used as a first name in the Orkneys.

William [will-ee-um]

Meaning: 'helmet of resolution', from the Old German elements 'will', 'volition' and 'helmet'.
William the Lion succeeded his brother Malcolm IV in 1165 and the name became popular in Scotland thereafter.

It became a surname in many guises: Wilson, Wilkinson, Wilkie, and so on.

Diminutives: Bill, Billy, Will, Willie

Gaelic cognate: Uilleam

Famous names: Billy Connolly, comedian; William Shakespeare, poet and playwright; William Wordsworth, poet; Will Carling, rugby player; Prince William, eldest son of Prince Charles and Diana, Princess of Wales.

GIRLS' FIRST NAMES

GIRLS' NAMES

Adamina [ad-u-mee-nu]
Meaning: 'red earth' in Hebrew.
A rare Scottish feminine form of ADAM, said to have originated in the eighteenth century. It was, according to the Gaelic fashion, the ecclesiastical name most resembling the Gaelic name Aedh (fire).

Africa [af-ree-ku]
Meaning: possibly derived from the Gaelic *ath-breac* (somewhat speckled).
This name (which has nothing to do with the continent of Africa), was a popular Scottish Christian name in the twelfth century and continued in general use until the eighteenth century.
Variant spellings: Effric, Eatric, Affrica, Afreka
Gaelic cognate: Oighrig

Agnes [ag-nes]
Meaning: from the Greek for 'pure' or 'chaste'.
A Scottish name by adoption, but used mainly in Scotland in the twentieth century. It is sometimes used in reverse, as Senga.

One of the four virgin saints, Agnes shares the role as patroness of purity with St Barbara, St Katharine and St Margaret. St Agnes was a Roman maiden martyred in the early fourth century. Traditionally she was a girl of only thirteen who refused marriage because of her dedication to Christ. She preferred death to the violation of her virginity and was executed with a sword piercing her throat. Her emblem is a lamb.

In Scotland from the fourteenth century onwards, the name was associated with the Countess of March, known as Black Agnes, who made a spirited and successful defence of the castle of Dunbar against the English.

Variant spelling: Senga
Dimunitives: Aggie, Aggy, Nessa, Nessie, Annis, Agnesina
Gaelic cognate: Aigneas
Famous name: Agnes Moorhead, actress.

Aigneas. *See* AGNES

Aileas. *See* ALICE

Aileen [ay-leen]
Meaning: possibly derived from the Greek word for 'light'.
This is a form of the Irish name Eileen, which was brought to England and Scotland in the 1870s.

The name gained general popularity in Europe through association with Elene, the mother of the Roman emperor Constantine the Great.

Variant spellings: Eileen, Ayleen, Ilean, Ileene, Ilene, Eilean
Dimunitives: Eily, Eiley
Gaelic cognate: Eibhlin
See also HELEN

Ailidh. *See* ALICE

Ailie. *See* ALISON

Ailsa [ail-su]
Meaning: 'noble maiden' in Old German.
This is the Scottish form of Elsa. Ailsa Craig is an island rock at the mouth of the Firth of Clyde and the name was originally used as a first name in Scotland exclusively.

Ainslie [ains-lee]
Meaning: 'my meadow', derived from 'hermitage' and 'wood' in Old English.
　In Scotland it is used as a first name for both boys and girls.
Variant spellings: Aynslie, Ainsley

Alana [al-ar-nu]
Meaning: 'cheerful' in Latin, originally of Celtic origin.
This is the feminine form of ALAN, peculiar to Scotland.
Variant spellings: Allana, Alaine, Alena, Alina, Alayne, Alayna

Alexis [al-ex-iss]
Meaning: 'helper' in Greek.
St Alexis lived by begging. On his death in 430 he was identified by documents in his handwriting, by voices from heaven and by miracles.
　It was discovered that he was a Roman nobleman who left his wife on his wedding day to live in poverty in Syria.
　Originally a boy's name, Alexis is now used exclusively as a girl's name in Scotland.

Alice [al-iss]
Meaning: from the Old German for 'nobility'.
The name was brought to England by the Normans and commonly used in the Middle Ages. After the publication of *Alice in Wonderland* by Lewis Carroll it became one of the

most popular names.
Variant spellings: Alicia, Alys, Alycia, Alissa
Dimunitives: Ailie, Ellie, Ailidh (Aileas]
Gaelic cognate: Aileas
Famous name: Alice Fay, actress; Alice Walker, author.

Alina [a-lin-u]
Meaning: defender of men.
Used in Scotland as a feminine form of ALASDAIR. It also resembles the Gaelic word *alainn* (lovely), which may account for its return to popularity.
Variant spellings: Allina, Aline

Alison [al-li-son]
Meaning: 'nobility' in Old German.
Originally the French dimunitive of Alice, in Scotland the name overtook Alice in popularity. It appears in medieval English poems as Alisoun. Chaucer's Alisoun, in *The Millers Tale*, is said to be more pleasant to look on than a flowering pear tree.

It has been a popular name in Scotland since the thirteenth century.
Variant spellings: Allison, Allyson, Alisanne, Alyson, Alisoun, Alysoun, Alysanne
Dimunitives: Allie, Ally, and Ailie (particularly popular in Scotland)
Gaelic cognate: Allasan
Famous names: Alison Lurie, novelist; Alison Steadman, actress.

Alissa. *See* ALICE

Allana. *See* ALANA

Allasun. *See* ALISON

Allena. *See* ALANAS

Allina. *See* ALINA

Allison. *See* ALISON

Allyson. *See* ALISON

Alys. *See* ALICE

Alyson. *See* ALISON

Anabal. *See* ANNABEL

Andrea [an-dree-ha]
Meaning: feminine form of ANDREW, which means 'manly'.
In Scotland it was common practice to form a girl's name by
adding *-ena* or *-ina* to a boy's name.
Variant spellings: Andreana, Andrewina, Andriene, Andrine,
Andrene, Andrianna, Andreena, Andrean, Dreena, Rena,
Andrena

Angusina [ang-us-eena]
Meaning: 'unique choice'.
Feminine form of ANGUS.

Anna [an-nu]
Meaning: favour or grace in Greek.
This is a Gaelic name popularized by biblical references to
Anne, the mother of the Virgin Mary. Ann and Anne are the
French and English forms which are frequently used as

middle names rather than first names, for example Margaret Ann.

The use of the name goes back to pre-Christian times. Anna is the sister of Dido, queen of Carthage in Virgil's *Aeneid*. It occurs in Christian inscriptions from the sixth century, and the Apocryphal Gospels name Anna (St Ann), wife of Joachim as the mother of the Virgin Mary. A church in Constantinople was built in her honour by Justinian I and relics were taken from it to Jerusalem and Rome. Her feast day, the Conception of St Anne, was celebrated at Canterbury from c. 1100.

In art, St Anne is often depicted as teaching the Virgin to read.

Variant spellings: Ann, Anne, Annette
Dimunitive: Nan
Famous names: Anna Pavlova, ballerina; Anna Neagle, actress; Anna Massey, actress; Annette Crosbie, actress; Anne Boleyn, second wife of Henry VIII; Anne of Cleves, fourth wife of Henry VIII.

Annabel [an-nu-bel]
Meaning: possibly derived from the Latin for 'lovable'.

This name, which is too ancient to be derived from Ann, possibly came from Aine (joy), a favourite name in early Gaelic times.

Alternatively, Annabelle may have been intended to mean ANNA, the beautiful one. A clue to the former pronunciation of the name is given by Annaple, the name given by Sir Walter Scott to characters in two of his novels, *The Heart of Midlothian* and *The Black Dwarf*.

Variant spellings: Annabelle, Anabel, Anabella, Annabella
Gaelic cognate: Anabal
Famous name: Annabel Drummond, mother of James I.

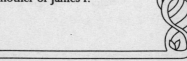

Annaple. *See* ANNABEL

Arabella [arr-u-bell-u]
Meaning: from 'moved by prayer' in Latin.
Originally a Scottish medieval name, it is now in common use.

The grand-daughter of William the Lion of Scotland was called Arabella, and Arabella Stuart died as a prisoner in the Tower of London in 1615. The name became very well known in 1712 when Alexander Pope published his poem, *The Rape of the Lock*. This was based on a true incident when Lord Petre forcibly cut off a lock of hair belonging to Arabella Fermor.

The name gained popularity in the mid-nineteenth century, as the result of its associationn with Arabella Allen, a character in Charles Dickens' *The Pickwick Papers*.
Variant spellings: Belle, Bella, Arabelle
Famous names: Arabella Boxer, cookery writer.

Ayleen. *See* AILEEN

Barabal. *See* BARBARA

Barbara [bar-bu-ru]
Meaning: the feminine form of 'stranger' or 'foreigner' in Greek.
St Barbara, who with St Margaret, St Agnes and St Katharine is one of the four virgin saints, was alleged to have been killed in the persecution of Maximian. She is the patron saint of architects and engineers and is invoked as protection against thunder and lightning, accidents and sudden death.

According to legend, she was imprisoned in a high tower by her father, who on discovering her secret conversion to Christianity, beheaded her. He was then struck down by a bolt of lightning. Angels descended and carried the girl's head to Paradise while devils took her father down to the bottomless pit.

The name, in the form of such surnames such as Babbe, Babbs and Barbe, has been used since the thirteenth or fourteenth centuries.
Variant spellings: Babra, Barbra
Dimunitives: Baubie, Babs, Barbie
Gaelic cognate: Barabal
Famous names: Barbara Dixon, singer; Barbara Windsor, actress; Barbara Trapido, novelist; Barbra Streisand, actress.

Baubie. *See* BARBARA

Bearnas. *See* BERENICE

Beathag [beh-ak]
Meaning: 'offspring of life' in Celtic.
This is the feminine form of BEATHAN and a name with ancient royal associations, having been given to the

daughters of Malcolm II and Donald Bane (Donald III). In official documents written in Latin, Beatrice was sometimes used as an alternative.

Beatrice [bee-triss]
Meaning: 'bringer of happiness' in Latin.
Beatrice was a medieval saint who was martyred with her two brothers, Simplicius and Faustinus. Her brothers were apparently put to death for refusing to sacrifice to the pagan gods. A neighbour denounced Beatrice for burying them. She was strangled in prison and buried with her brothers.

Her name was originally Viatrix (traveller) and the name was adopted by the early Christians in reference to the journey through life and the way, the life and the truth. It was later altered as a result of association with the Latin *beatus*, meaning blessed.

Beatrice was a popular name in Scotland during the Middle Ages. It is recorded in the Domesday Book.
Variant spelling: Beatrix
Dimunitives: Bea, Beattie, Trixie, Breatty
Gaelic cognate: Beitris
Famous names: Princess Beatrice of the Netherlands; Beatrix Potter, children's writer and illustrator

Beitiris. *See* BEATRICE

Bella. *See* ARABELLA, ISOBEL

Berenice [ber-e-nees]
Meaning: 'bringer of victory' in Greek.
The name was popular in Ancient Greece and Rome, and in the New Testament Berenice was the daughter of Herod Agrippa.

It was introduced to Britain after the Reformation.
Gaelic cognate: Bearnas

Bernadette [ber-na-det]
Meaning: 'brave as a bear' or 'stern'.
The feminine form of BERNARD. It became well known when Bernadette Soubirous experienced several visions of the Virgin Mary in 1858 at a grotto in Lourdes, southern France.
Famous name: Bernadette Devlin, politician.

Bessie. *See* ELIZABETH

Beth [beth]
Meaning: from 'life' in Celtic.
The name was introduced to Scotland from Ireland. A legendary Irish princess, Bega, became a nun and founded the nunnery of St Bees in Cumbria. Although it is often considered a pet form of Elizabeth, it is a name in its own right. Macbeth is derived from the same Celtic word.

Betty. *See* ELIZABETH

Bonnie [bon-nee]
Meaning: 'good' in Latin.
This is the short form of Bonita, and also the Scottish term for pretty.
It is now used as a first name, made especially popular by the films *Gone with the Wind* and *Bonnie and Clyde*.
Famous name: Bonnie Langford, actress.

Brenda [bren-du]
Meaning: possibly from 'sword' in Old Norse.

Brought to Shetland by Norsemen, Brenda was an established name in Scotland from early times. Its popularity increased when Sir Walter Scott used it as the name for one of his two heroines in his novel *The Pirate*, which was set in the coastal areas of the Shetlands.
Famous name: Brenda Blethin, actress

Bride. *See* BRIDGET

Bridget [brij-it]
Meaning: 'high one' or 'strength' in Celtic.
Brighde was the Celtic goddess of poetry and fertility. She is identified with St Brighde of Kildare, the pupil of St Patrick. She founded the monastery of Kildare, the first religious house of women in Ireland and contributed to the spread of Christianity. Her cult spread to England and Scotland, where churches were dedicated to her under the medieval form of her name, St Bride.
Variant spelling: Bridie
Gaelic cognates: Brighde, Bride
Famous name: Bridget Brophy, novelist.

Brighde. *See* BRIDGET

Catristiona. *See* CATHERINE

Catherine [kath-u-rin]
Meaning: 'pure' in Greek.
St Catherine of Alexandria was a beautiful and intelligent virgin of noble descent who, on rejecting Maximian, was tortured by being bound between spiked wheels. She was then beheaded.

The name became popular in the West after the Crusades, and even more so in the nineteenth century, when Robert Louis Stephenson published his novel *Catriona*.

Catherine is the patron saint of young girls, students and nurses, and craftsmen whose work is based on the wheel.
Variant spellings: Caterina, Caitir, Katrina
Dimunitives: Riona, Katie, Katy
Gaelic cognate: Catriona (often used in Scotland).
Famous names: Catherine of Aragon, first wife of Henry VIII; Catherine Howard, fifth wife of Henry VIII; Catherine Parr, sixth wife of Henry VIII; Catherine Cookson, novelist; Kate Bush, singer; Kate Moss, model; Katie Stewart, cookery writer.

Catriona. *See* CATHERINE, KATRINE

Cecilia [se-*See*-lee-u]
Meaning: derived from the Latin for 'blind'.
An early Christian martyr, Cecilia is the patron saint of musicians.
Variant spellings: Cecily, Cecelia, Cicely
Masculine form: Cecil
Gaelic cognate: Sile
Famous names: Cecily Mary Barker, poet and artist; Cecily Courtney, actress.

Christina [kris-tee-nu]
Meaning: 'follower of Christ' in Latin.
The name was that of a Roman virgin martyred in Bolsena in 295, and was brought to Scotland by Queen Margaret in the eleventh century. She was the daughter of the king of Denmark and Norway and married James III. Christina was a popular name in her country of origin.
Variant spellings: Christine, Christiana, Kirsten
Dimunitives: Chris, Chrissie, Christie; Kirstie and Kirsty are pet names in Scotland.
Masculine form: Christian
Gaelic cognates: Cairistiona, Ciorstaidh, Kirsty
Famous names: Chris Evert, tennis player; Kirsty Young, radio presenter.

Ciorstaidh. *See* CATHERINE

Clemintina [klem-in-tee-na]
Meaning: 'mild' or 'merciful' in Latin.
The feminine form of Clement, made famous by the song, 'My Darling Clementine'.
Variant spelling: Clementine
Gaelic cognate: Climidh
Famous name: Clementine Spencer Churchill, wife of Sir Winston Churchill.

Dallas [dal-las]
Meaning: 'water meadow'.
This Scottish place name, Dallas, in Elginshire, is also a surname and is now used as a first name for both boys and girls.

Davida. *See* DAVINA

Davidina. *See* DAVINA

Davina [du-vee-nu]
Meaning: 'beloved' or 'darling'.
This is the feminine form of DAVID, a very popular name in Scotland.
Variant spellings: Davidina, Davida, Davinia, Divinia, Vida, Vidette

Dearbhail. *See* DOROTHY

Dodie. *See* DOROTHY

Doileag. *See* DOLINA

Dolina [doll-ee-nu]
Meaning: 'proud ruler'.
The feminine of DONALD.
Variant spellings: Donella, Donalda, Donaldina, Dona
Gaelic cognate: Doileag

Donalda. *See* DOLINA

Donella. *See* DOLINA

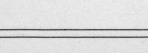

Dora. *See* DOROTHY

Dorcas [dor-cas]
Meaning: from 'gazelle' in Greek.
In the New Testament, Dorcas (the Greek translation of Tabitha) is a woman well known for her charitable acts, and raised from the dead by St Peter. The name's biblical origins account for its popularity, especially among the Puritans in the sixteenth and seventeenth centuries.

Later, Dorcas was the name given to a meeting of ladies to make clothes for the poor.

Dorothy [dor-o-thee]
Meaning: 'gift of God' in Greek.
St Dorothy was martyred in the time of Diocletian. On the way to her execution a man mocked her and asked her to send him a gift of fruit and flowers from heaven. A small child immediately appeared and gave him a basket of apples and roses.

The name has been used in Britain since the fifteenth century. It had become so common by the next century that its dimunitive, Doll, became a word for the child's toy.
Variant spellings: Dorothea, Dora
Dimunitives: Dot, Dolly, Dottie, Dodie, Doll
Gaelic cognate: Dearbhail
Famous names: Dorothy Sayers, author; Dora Carrington, painter; Dolly Parton, country and western singer; Dodie Stephens, author.

Dot. *See* DOROTHY

Douglasina [dug-las-ee-na]
Meaning: 'dark water'.
A rare name, the feminine form of DOUGLAS, only used in
Scotland. It was originally a place name and surname taken
from the river Douglas.

The name Douglas can be used as a first name for both
boys and girls.

Dreena. *See* ANDREW

Eafric. *See* AFRICA

Ealasaid. *See* ELIZABETH

Eamag. *See* EMILY

Eapag. *See* EUPHEMIA

Edme. *See* ESME

Edwina [ed-wee-nu]
Meaning: 'prosperous friend' in Old English.
This name, the feminine form of Edwin, is more common in
Scotland than elsewhere.
Variant spellings: Edweena, Edwena, Edwyna
Famous names: Edwina Currie, politician; Edwina, Lady
Mountbatten, wife of Lord Mountbatten of Burma.

Effie. *See* EUPHEMIA

Effric. *See* AFRICA

Egidia. *See* GILES

EibhlinI. *See* AILEEN and HELEN

Eileen. *See* AILEEN

Eilidh. *See* HELEN

Eilispidh. *See* ELIZABETH

Eily. *See* AILEEN

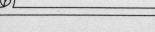

Elaine [e-layn]
Meaning: from the Greek for 'light'.
This is the Old French form of HELEN.

Two women named Elaine feature in Arthurian legend. One fell in love with Sir Lancelot and assumed the form of Guinevere for one night. Their union resulted in the birth of Sir Galahad. The other died of unrequited love for Sir Lancelot.

In Scotland in the 1950s Elaine replaced Ellen in popularity.
Variant spellings: Ellaine, Elaina, Elayne
Famous names: Elaine Page, singer; Elaine Stritch, actress.

Elizabeth [ee-liz-u-beth]
Meaning: from the Hebrew for 'God is generous' or 'God is perfection'.
This name owes its popularity to its biblical origins. In 1978 one Scottish woman in twenty-four bore this name.

In the Old Testament Elizabeth, the wife of Aaron, gave birth to John the Baptist when she was an old woman.

St Elizabeth of Hungary (1207–1231) was especially popular in Europe. Born a princess, she was happily married and spent much money on the care of children and orphans. After her husband, Louis, died of the plague in the Crusades, she became a Franciscan tertiary and devoted herself to the sick and needy. Her niece, Elizabeth of Portugal, named after her, pursued a life of prayer and piety and on becoming a widow, she also devoted herself to the sick and needy.

These two saints contributed to the popularity of the name in the Middle Ages.
Variant spellings: Elspeth, Elspet, Elisabeth, Bess

Dimunitives: Bessie, Beth, Betty, Eliza, Elspie, Elsbeth, Elsie, Elspeth, Lillibet, Lisa, Lizbeth. Many of these dimunitives are names in their own right.
Gaelic cognates: Ealasaid, Eilispidh
Famous names: Elizabeth I, queen of England and Ireland; Elizabeth II, queen of Great Britain and Northern Ireland; Elizabeth Barrett Browning, author and poet; Liz Hurley, film actress; Betty Boothroyd, the Speaker of the House of Commons; Elspeth Davie, author; Elizabeth Taylor, actress.

Ella. *See* ISOBEL

Ellaine. *See* ELAINE

Ellen. *See* ELAINE and HELEN

Elsie. *See* ELIZABETH

Elspeth. *See* ELIZABETH

Emily [em-i-lee]
Meaning: from the Latin for 'eager'.
Derived from a Roman clan name Aemilius, this was a popular name among the early Christians.
    Geoffrey Chaucer named a character Emelye in his *The Knights Tale*. It began to be used as a first name in Scotland in the nineteenth century.
Gaelic cognate: Eamag
Famous names: Emily Brontë, author; Emily Davis, founder of Girton College, Cambridge; Emily Dickinson, poet.

Ena. *See* INA

Ephie. *See* EUPHEMIA

Erica [er-i-cu]
Meaning: from the Old Norse for 'one ruler'.
This name, the feminine form of Eric, remains popular in Scotland.

Although it is associated with heather (an *erica*), this is not the true source of the name.
Variant spelling: Erika
Famous name: Erica Jong, author.

Esme [es-mee]
Meaning: 'to esteem' in Old French.
Originally a boy's name, it was introduced to Scotland from France in the sixteenth century by Esmé Stewart dAubigny, Duke of Lennox and cousin of James VI, whose mother was French.

Euphemia [eu-fee-mee-u]
Meaning: 'fair speech' or 'well spoken for' in Greek.
Because the name also means abstinence from speech, it signifies silence, applied to the stillness during religious rites.

The name occurs in the New Testament, in the Acts of the Apostles. Euphemia is one of the four concubines of Agrippa, who were converted to Christianity and suffered death for their chastity. St Euphemia was a virgin martyr of Bithynia, whom the lions in the arena refused to devour. Her constancy, unshaken and invulnerable to lions or to flames, became a legend.

The name was especially popular in the nineteenth century, as it was thought to translate the Gaelic name Oighrig.

Dimunitives: Effie, Fanny, Phemie, Ephie, Euphan, Euphen
Gaelic cognate: Eapag
Famous name: Fanny Burney, novelist; Fanny Craddock, chef and cookery writer.

Fanny. *See* EUPHEMIA

Fenella [fen-el-lu]
Meaning: 'white shoulder'.
Sir Walter Scott used the name Fenella in his novel *Peveril of the Peak*. However, the character is severely handicapped and it is thought that perhaps this is the reason the name was of limited popularity in Scotland.
Variant spellings: Finella, Fionola, Finola, Fionnuala
Gaelic cognate: Fionnaghal
Famous name: Fenella Fielding, actress.

Fiona [fyo-nu]
Meaning: 'white girl' in Celtic, or 'fair' in Gaelic.
This name was invented by William Sharp (1855–1905), the Scottish author. Fiona MacLeod was the pseudonym under which he wrote a series of tales and romances based on ancient Celtic folklore. Consequently the name was used mainly in Scotland, and is thought of as a Scottish name.
Famous name: Fiona Pitt-Kethley, poet

Fionnaghul. *See* FENELLA

Fionnuala. *See* FENELLA

Floireans. *See* FLORENCE

Flora [flor-u]
Meaning: 'flower' in Latin.
This is the name of the Roman goddess of flowers and spring. In Scotland it is sometimes used in place of the Gaelic name, Fionnaghul, although this is an informal association.

Flora Macdonald (1722–90) made the name famous. She helped Bonnie Prince Charlie to escape to the Isle of Skye after his defeat at Culloden.

Dimunitive: Florrie
Gaelic cognate: Floraidh

Floraidh. *See* FLORA

Florence [floh-runs]
Meaning: from the Latin for 'flourishing'.
After St Florentins was martyred in the third century, this became a popular name for both boys and girls.

Florence, the name of the great Tuscan city, has sometimes been used for someone who comes from Florence.

Florence Nightingale received her name because she was born there. Her fame ensured the continued popularity of the name for girls.

Variant spelling: Florance
Dimunitives: Flo, Florie, Flossie, Floy
Gaelic cognate: Floireans
Famous name: Florence Nightingale, nurse.

Florrie. *See* FLORA

Frances [fran-sis]
Meaning: from the Latin for 'Frenchman'.
The feminine form of FRANCIS, and popular in Scotland.

Variant spellings: Francesca, Francina, Franca, Frankie, Fran
Gaelic cognate: Frangag
Famous names: Frances Burnett, author; Frances Parkinson Keyes, author; Frances Wilkes, author.

Freya [frae-u]

Of Nordic origin, Freya, or Froja, was the goddess of love in Scandinavian mythology. She travelled in a chariot drawn by cats and wept tears of gold when her husband, Odin, was away. From Norway the name spread to the Shetlands and then Scotland.

Famous name: Freya Stark, author.

Georgina [jor-jee-nu]
Meaning: 'farmer' or 'husbandman'.
The feminine form of GEORGE. Early in the twentieth century Georgina was a decidely Scottish name in terms of usage, and has been popular since the eighteenth century.
Variant spellings: Georgia, Georgine, Georgette, Georgena
Dimunitive: Gina
Gaelic cognate: Seorsag
Famous name: Georgina Starr, actress.

Giles [jiles]
Meaning: from the Greek word for 'kid'.
Once used for both boys and girls, Giles was especially popular as a girl's name in the Edinburgh area, as St Giles is the patron of the city.

It is rarely used as a girl's name today. In Scotland, from about the sixteenth century, the name was always given to girls, sometimes in the Latin form, Egidia. Miss Egidia was chieftainess of the Menzies clan.

Grace [graes]
Meaning: from the Latin word *gratia* (grace).
This was the name of a Christian in fourth-century Rome, and was taken up by the Puritans in the seventeenth century. It had religious connotations, being associated with the phrase 'by the grace of God' and with the practice of saying grace before meals.

The name was popular in Scotland, particularly in the nineteenth century. This may have been by association with Grace Darling, a lighthouse keeper's daughter on one of the Farne Islands. In 1838 she and her father rescued nine people in dangerous seas, when the *Forfarshire* was wrecked off the Longstone lighthouse.

Dimunitives: Gracie, Gracey
Gaelic cognate: Giorsal
Famous names: Gracie Fields, singer and actress; Grace Kelly, actress, also titled Princess Grace of Monaco.

Gracie. *See* GRACE

Griselda [gri-zel-du]
Meaning: this is the Scottish contraction of Griseldis, which means 'grey battle-maid' in Old German.

Chaucer told the story of the patient Griselda in *The Clerk's Tale*. Her husband tried her patience in different ways, even taking her children from her to be brought up by foster parents. He told her that he had killed them. Later he brought home a beautiful young lady and told Griselda he was going to divorce her and marry the young woman. Griselda made no protest and only then did he reveal that the young woman was their daughter. The patience of Griselda became proverbial in the Middle Ages.
Variant spellings: Grizzell, Grizel (the most popular form in Scotland), Grissel, Grissell
Dimunitive: Zelda
Famous name: Zelda Fitzgerald, wife of F. Scott Fitzgerald

Grizel. *See* GRISELDA

Helen [hel-in]
Meaning: 'sun' in Celtic or 'light' in Greek.
In Greek legend, Helen was 'the face that launched a thousand ships'. The wife of Menelaus, she was abducted by Paris and carried off to Troy, thereby causing the Trojan War. On Paris' death, she married his brother then betrayed him to the Greeks and became reconciled with Menelaus.

St Helena was the mother of the Emperor Constantine. According to some legends she was British, either the daughter of an innkeeper or the daughter of Old King Cole of the nursery rhyme. She became a devout Christian at the age of sixty, gave generously to the poor and made a pilgrimage to the Holy Land. It is said that she played a part in the finding of the True Cross in Jerusalem in 335, where it was collected fragment by fragment.

'Burd Helen' is renowned in Scottish ballad lore for her resolute constancy.
Variant spellings: Ellen, Helena, Helene
Dimunitives: Lena, Nellie
Gaelic cognates: Eibhlin, Eilidh, Neillidh
Famous names: Helen Keller, campaigner on behalf of the blind; Helen Reddy, singer; Helena Bonham-Carter, actress.

Helena. *See* HELEN

Hilary [hil-ar-ee]
Meaning: 'hilarity' or 'cheerfulness'.
It is a name used for both boys and girls.
Variant spellings: Hillary, Hillery
Famous name: Hillary Rodham Clinton, lawyer and wife of President Bill Clinton.
See also HILARY (in Boys' Names)

Hughina [hew-ee-nu]
Meaning: heart or mind.
This is the feminine version of HUGH, and occurs mainly in
Scotland.

Ileene. *See* AILEEN

Ina [ee-na] or [eye-na]
This is the short form of a number of names ending in *ina*. In Scotland *-ina* is often added to a boy's name to make a girl's name; for example, Davina, Andrewina, Hughina. It is also a name in its own right.
Variant spelling: Ena

Inga
One of the names introduced into Shetland by Scandinavian settlers, it remained popular in Scotland. It is the short form of many other names including Ingeborg, Ingegard and Ingrid.
Famous name: Ingrid Bergman, actress.

Ingrid. *See* INGA

Innes [in-nis]
Meaning: 'island' in Greek.
It is the name of an island which became a surname and then later a clan name. It can be used as a first name for both girls and boys.

Iona [eye-oh-nu]
Meaning: 'violet-coloured stone' in Greek.
Iona is the name of the small Hebridean island on which St Columba founded a monastery, and from where he sent missionaries throughout Scotland. It is now used as a girl's name.

Iosbail. *See* ISOBEL

Isa. *See* ISOBEL

Iseabail. *See* ISOBEL

Ishbel. *See* ISOBEL

Isla [eye-lu]
Meaning: from 'the island' in French.
The name of a Scottish river, now used as a first name.
Famous name: Isla St Clair, television presenter.

Isobel [iz-o-bel]
Meaning: oath of God in Hebrew.
This is the preferred Scottish spelling of Isabel, a variant of ELIZABETH that probably originated from Scotlands alliance with France.

The name seems to have early origins in Provence. It became widely used in Spain and France, and until the sixteenth century Isabel and Elizabeth were interchangeable.

The fact that three queens of England were called Isabella – the wives of King John, Edward II and Richard II – contributed to its currency.
Variant spellings: Isabel, Isabelle, Ishbel, Isbel
Dimunitives: Isa, Bella, Ella, Tibbie (a nickname common in the Lowlands).
Gaelic cognates: Iseabail, Iosbail, Isbeal
Famous names: Dame Isobel Baillie, soprano; Isobel Black, actress; Isabella Rossellini, actress.

Ivy [eye-vee]
A Victorian name, from the plant, and used as a first name from the 1860s. In Scotland it is both a girl's and a boy's name.
Famous name: Dame Ivy Compton-Burnett, novelist.

Jacobina [jae-kob-ee-nu]
Meaning: supplanter.
A Scottish girl's name coined as the feminine form of JACOB. Its use in Scotland was widespread in the eighteenth century, when it was commonly bestowed by Jacobites. Jacoba and Jacobina were the names given to their daughters to demonstrate their loyalty to the Stuarts.
Variant spelling: Jacoba

Jamesina [ja-mis-eye-na]
Meaning: supplanter.
A feminine form of JAMES used in Scotland.

Jane [jain]
Meaning: 'God is Gracious'.
It is a form of the Latin Johanna, and the earlier Joan, as well as the feminine form of Johannes (John). Joanna (from whom the name Jane is derived) was a holy woman in the Bible.
Variant spellings: Jayne, Jaine, Jean
Dimunitives: Janell, Janene, JANET, Janetta, Janey, Janice, Janina, Janine, Janis, Janise, Janita
Gaelic cognate: Sine. This is usually spelt phonetically as Sheena.
Famous names: Jane Austen, author; Sheena Easton, pop singer; Jane Seymour, third wife of Henry VIII; Joan Baez, folk singer; Joan Sutherland, opera singer; Joanna Lumley, actress; Jane Asher, actress and cookery writer; Jane Fonda, actress.

Janet [jan-net]
Meaning: from the Hebrew meaning 'God is Gracious'.
A dimunitive of JANE, Janet is now a name in its own right. In the nineteenth century Janet was mainly a Scottish name.

Variant spellings: Janette; and the pet forms Jess, Jessie, Jennie and Jenny.
Dimunitives: Netta, Nita
Gaelic cognate: Seonaid
Famous names: Janet Baker, opera singer; Janet Brown, comedienne.

Janice. *See* JANE

Jean [jeen]
Meaning: 'God is Gracious'.
Feminine form of JOHN, this Scottish variant of JANE and JOAN is used as an independent name.
Dimunitives: Jeanie, Jeannie, Jeanette are all used as independent names.
Famous name: Jean Alexander, actress; Jean Muir, fashion designer; Jean Simmonds, actress; Jeanette MacDonald, actress and singer

Jeanette. *See* JEAN

Jemima [jem-eye-mu]
Meaning: 'dove' in Hebrew.
In the Old Testament, Jemima was one of the daughters of Job, all renowned for their beauty.

The name's biblical associations made it popular with the Puritans. It was also used by Sir Walter Scott as the name for a character in his story *My Aunt Margaret's Mirror*.
Gaelic associate: Simeog

Jennie. *See* JANET

Jessica. *See* JESSIE

Jessie [jes-*See*]
Meaning: 'God is looking' in Hebrew.
This shortened form of Jessica, or pet form of JANET, is also used as a name in its own right.
Variant spelling: Jessye
Gaelic cognates: Seasaidh, Teasaidh
Famous name: Jessye Norman, opera singer.

Joan. *See* JANE

Joanna. *See* JANE

Johanna. *See* JANE

Joyce [joy-is]
Meaning: from the Latin *jocosa* (merry).
It can be used as both a girl's and a boy's name. In 1885 Edna Lyall used it as the name of her heroine in the novel, *In the Golden Days*, helping to revive its popularity.
Famous name: Joyce Grenfell, author and actress.
See also JOYCE (in Boys' Names)

Julia [juw-lee-u]
Meaning: 'downy' or 'mossy-bearded'.
This is a feminine form of Julius, said to be a Roman clan name.
Sileas of Keppoch, Lochaber (1660–1729) was a MacDonald poetess who lived in Banffshire. In recent times Julie has been the more usual form of this name in Scotland.
Variant spelling: Julie
Gaelic cognate: Sileas

Famous names: Julia Somerville, television presenter; Julie Andrews, actress; Julie Walters, actress; Julie Christie, actress; Julia Margaret Cameron, photographer.

Julie. *See* JULIA

Katie. *See* CATHERINE

Katrina. *See* CATHERINE

Katrine [kat-reen]
Meaning: 'band of peasants'.
This name, which originated in the 1870s, is the name of a
loch in the Trossachs.
Variant spelling: Catriona.

Kirsty. *See* CHRISTINA

Kyle [keye-il]
Meaning: from the Gaelic for 'channel between islands' or
'handsome'.
Although more commonly known as a place name in the
Kyles of Bute, between the Scottish coast and the island of
Bute, this name is also a surname and first name for both
boys and girls.
See also KYLE (in Boys' Names)

Lena. *See* HELEN

Lennox [len-ox]
Meaning: 'an abundance of elm trees'.
This Scottish place name and aristocratic surname is also a first name both for boys and girls.
Variant spelling: Lenox

Lesley [lez-lee]
Meaning: possibly from the Gaelic for 'low-lying meadow' or 'garden by a pond'.
Originally a place name (Leslie, in Aberdeenshire) and a surname, it is now also a first name for boys and girls. Lesley was established as a feminine form when the name was used by Robert Burns in his poem, *Bonnie Lesley*.
Variant spellings: Leslie, Leslee, Lesli, Leslye, Lesly, Lesslie
Diminutive: Les
Famous name: Leslie Carson, actress.
See also LESLIE (in Boys' Names)

Lileas. *See* LILLIAS

Lilidh. *See* LILLIAS

Lillian [lil-ee-un]
Meaning: from the Latin for 'lily'.
According to legend, the lily sprang from the tears of Eve, as she was driven out of the Garden of Eden. In Christian art the lily is a symbol of purity.
Variant spellings: Lilias, Lillian, Lily, Lillah
Gaelic cognates: Lilidh, Lileas
Famous names: Lily Langtry, actress, socialite and mistress of Edward VII; Lillian Beckwith, author; Lillian Gish, actress.

Lillias. *See* LILLIAN

Lily. *See* LILLIAN

Lindsey [lind-see]
Meaning: 'of gentle speech' in Old German or a Scottish place name meaning 'Lellis island'.
Variant spellings: Lindsay, Linsey, Lyndsey, Lysey
See also LINDSAY (in Boys' Names)

Lisa. *See* ELIZABETH

Liusaidh. *See* LUCY

Lorn [lorn]
Meaning: derived from the Celtic word *lovernos* (fox).
Latharn was the name of the founder of Cineal Lathairn, one of the three main regions of the Scottish Kingdom of Dalriada. He is commemorated in the district name of Latharna (Lorn) in Argyll.
Variant spelling: Lorne
Gaelic cognate: Latharn

Lorna [lor-nu]
Meaning: 'love lorn' or 'love lost' in Anglo-Saxon.
This name, based on the place name LORN, was invented by R.D. Blackmore for the heroine of his romantic novel *Lorna Doone* (1869).

This novel is set on Exmoor, where an outlawed family, the Doones, terrorize the surrounding countryside. John Ridd, the hero of the story, discovers Lorna, a young girl living with the Doones, and they grow up and fall in love. They discover that Lorna has been kidnapped, and is really

Lady Lorna Dugal, of the MacDougalls of Lorne. John Ridd is a rival for Lorna's hand with Carver Doone, from whom he rescues her in a severe blizzard. At John and Lorna's wedding Carver Doone shoots her at the altar. John revenges her but is harmed himself. Carver dies and eventually both Lorna and John recover.

Lorraine [lorr-aen]

The name is derived from Jeanne la Lorraine, or JOAN of Arc, who was born in 1411 at Domrèmy, Lorraine, in north-eastern France. Its association with Joan of Arc (St Joan) and with MARY of Lorraine, mother of Mary Queen of Scots, probably accounts for its popularity as a first name.

Lorraine, Lorain and Lorain are all Scottish surnames, and probably indicate that the original bearers of the name came from that part of France.

Variant spellings: Loraine, Lorain, Lorayne, Lorane
Famous name: Lorraine Kelly, television presenter.

Lucille. *See* LUCY

Lucinda. *See* LUCY

Lucy [loo-see]

Meaning: from the Latin for 'light' or 'dawn'.

The name was often used for a child born at daybreak. The virgin martyr, St Lucy, was a popular saint in the Middle Ages and her name was used throughout Britain.

She was a wealthy Sicilian who refused marriage and gave her possessions to the poor and needy. She was accused by her suitor and found guilty. She remained miraculously immovable when they attempted to have her violated. They were also unsuccessful in having her burnt, so eventually she was killed by the sword. Her fame is based on these acts and her eyes, which were reputed to have been torn out and miraculously restored, are her emblem. She is the patron saint of the blind and those suffering from diseases of the eye.

Sir Walter Scott named his bride Lucy in his novel *The Bride of Lammermoor*, but as she died insane it did not encourage the use of Lucy as a first name.

Variant spellings: Lucinda, Luce, Lucille

Gaelic cognate: Liusaidh

Famous names: Lucinda Lambton, author and television presenter; Lucy Ellman, novelist; Lucille Ball, actress.

Mabel [may-bull]
Meaning: possibly 'my beautiful one', from the French *ma belle*.
Originally a pet form of Amabel, it is now a name in its own right. An old form, Mabella, is sometimes found in Scotland.

In 1946, Lewis Grassic Gibson published *A Scots Quair*, a trilogy written in lyrical prose with use of Scottish dialect and archaisms, in which there is reference to a 'Quean called Mabel'.
Variant spelling: Mable, Maybel, Maybelle
Famous name: Mabel Lucy Attwell, writer and illustrator of children's books.

Maidie. *See* MARY

Maighsi. *See* MARGARET

Maili. *See* MARY

Mairead. *See* MARGARET

Mairi. *See* MARY

Maisie. *See* MARGARET

Margaret [mar-gu-ret]
Meaning: possibly from the Greek for 'pearl'.
In Persian the name means 'child of light', following the belief that pearls are formed from dew touched by moonbeams.

It became popular in eastern Europe because of the third-century martyr, St Margaret of Antioch, and in Scotland was made even more popular because of St Margaret of Scotland (1046–93).

She was one of the last members of the Anglo-Saxon royal family and after the Norman Conquest took refuge at the court of Malcolm III, King of Scotland, and married him in 1069. Beautiful, pious and cultured she was noted for her care of orphans and the poor. She was also a principal agent in the reform of the Church in Scotland. Her private life was devoted to prayer, reading, lavish almsgiving and ecclesiastical needlework. After her death she was buried beside her husband at Dunfermline, and later canonized.

Margaret has been called 'the national Scottish female name', and even in the 1980s about one girl in twenty born in Scotland was called Margaret.

Maisie was originally a Scottish pet form of Margaret, but can be used as a name in its own right. Mysie is another form of the name, and has appeared in the novels of Sir Walter Scott.

Variant spellings: Margo, Margarita, Marguerite, Margret
Diminutives: Meg, Maggie, Meggie, Maisie, Mysie, Peg, Peggy
Gaelic cognates: Maighsi, Mairead
Famous names: Margaret Drabble, author; Dame Margaret Rutherford, actress; Princess Margaret, sister of Queen Elizabeth II; Dame Margaret Thatcher, stateswoman; Dame Margot Fonteyn, ballerina; Peggy Mount, actress; Margot Hemingway, model; Meg Ryan, actress; Dame Peggy Ashcroft, actress.

Margery. *See* MARJORIE

Margo. *See* MARGARET

Marjorie [marj-or-ee]
Meaning: 'pearl'.
Originally a Scottish form of Margaret, but long used as an independent name. Marjorie was the daughter of Robert the Bruce. By her marriage to Walter the High Steward, she became the ancestress of the Stewart (Stuart) dynasty. Their son, Robert II, was the first of their family to wear the crown of Scotland.

This name has suffered since the introduction of margarine, the butter substitute, often abbreviated to 'marge'. In her novel *Female Friends*, Fay Weldon makes her character Marjorie say, 'I hated margarine. Everyone called me Marge at school.'
Variant spelling: Margery, Marjory
Diminutive: Marge
Gaelic cognate: Marsaili
Famous name: Margery Allingham, author.

Marsaili. *See* MARJORIE

Mary [mair-ree]
Meaning: 'wished-for child' in Hebrew.
Mary is the Greek form of Miriam. Its association with the Virgin Mary accounts for the name's popularity in Christian cultures, although it was originally considered too holy for such a use.

Mary, Queen of Scots is probably the best-known Scottish bearer of the name. Queen at one week old she was taken to France to escape the Protestants. She returned, married and was implicated in the murder of her husband. She was imprisoned for twenty years by Elizabeth I before being executed.

Loyal Scottish parents used the name frequently. Maidie is a Scottish pet form of Mary, or it can be an affectionate nickname for a maiden, or young girl.

Diminutives: Molly, Maidie, Moll
Gaelic cognates: Mairi, Maili
Famous names: Mary Riggans, actress; Mary Somerville, founder of Somerville College, Oxford; Mary I, queen of England; Molly Keane, novelist.

Maybelle. *See* MABEL

Meg. *See* MARGARET

Minna. *See* WILMA

Minnie [min-nee]
Meaning: 'pearl'.
This is a Scottish form of MARY, but it also has a distinct origin of its own. Troubadors in Germany in the twelfth and thirteenth centuries were called 'Minnesingers'.

Moira [moy-ru]
This phonetic form of the Irish name Maire is popular in Scotland, mainly since the beginning of the twentieth century.
Variant spelling: Moyra
Gaelic cognate: Moire
Famous names: Moira Shearer, ballet dancer; Moira Stewart, television newscaster; Moira Anderson, singer.

Molly. *See* MARY

Morag [mor-rag]
Meaning: the diminutive of the Gaelic *mor* (great or large).
This almost exclusively Scottish name was once thought to be the equivalent of SARAH.

When Bonnie Prince Charlie was in hiding, trying to make his way back to France, it was one of the titles used to refer to him, by his followers, when it was dangerous to mention his proper name.

Morna [morn-u]
Meaning: 'beloved' or 'gentle' in Gaelic.
Used almost solely in Scotland.
Variant spellings: Myrna, Moyna
Gaelic cognate: Muirne
Famous name: Myrna Loy, actress.

Morven [mor-ven]
Meaning: 'mountain peak' in Gaelic.
This place name has become a first name.

It is the name of two mountains in Grampian and Highland respectively (the former regions of Aberdeenshire and Caithness), and also the name of a district in the north-west Highlands.

In Macpherson's Ossianic poems (1765) Morven is used to represent the whole of north-west Scotland.
Variant spellings: Morvern, Morvyn

Muireall. *See* MURIEL

Muirne. *See* MORNA

Murdino [mur-dee-no]
Feminine form of MURDO, meaning 'sailor'.

Muriel [mew-ree-il]
Meaning: 'sea bright' or 'fair one of the sea' in Celtic.
The name might have been common to the Celtic languages
in early times. It was generally popular in the Middle Ages,
and gave rise to surnames such as Merrall and Murrell.

In 1493 the Nairnshire thaneship fell to an infant heiress,
Muriel. One of her guardians sent sixty of his clansmen to
kidnap the little girl when she was only four. A party set off
in pursuit of the kidnappers, and six of the Campbells were
killed trying to delay the pursuers, while the rest escaped
with the little girl. She eventually married Sir John
Campbell of Inverliver in 1501 and it led to the founding of
the Campbells of Calder (or Cawdor).
Gaelic cognate: Muireall
Famous names: Muriel Spark, author; Muriel Gray, television
presenter; Muriel Pavlov, actress.

Myrna. *See* MORNA

Mysie. *See* MARGARET

Nan. *See* ANNA

Neillidh. *See* HELEN

Nella. *See* FENELLA

Nellie. *See* HELEN

Nessie. *See* AGNES

Netta. *See* JANET

Nita. *See* JANET

Norma [nor-ma]
Meaning: 'pattern' or 'model' in Latin.
Especially popular in Scotland where it was considered to be
the feminine form of NORMAN.
Famous name: Norma Shearer, ballet dancer

Nuala. *See* FENELLA

Oighrig. *See* AFRICA

Olive [o-liv]
The name of the olive tree has been used for centuries as a first name, the olive being the symbol of peace. Religious connotations ensured the name's popularity.
Variant spelling: Olivia
Famous names: Olivia de Havilland, actress; Olivia Newton John, actress and singer.

Osla [os-lu]
Meaning: 'God consecrated' in Old Norse.
This was another name brought to Shetland and Scotland by the Norsemen. It is said that when girls bearing this name came to be christened they were often baptized with the similar-sounding name Ursula (little bear).

Patricia [pat-rish-u]
Meaning: 'noble' in Latin.
Patricia is the feminine form of the Latin name Patricius. It is used as the Scottish feminine form of PATRICK. It is first recorded in the sixth and the seventh centuries as the name of a nun, Patricia, patron saint of Naples.

It was infrequently used in English-speaking countries until the beginning of the twentieth century, when it was associated with Princess Patricia, granddaughter of Queen Victoria.
Diminutives: Pat, Tricia, Trisha
Famous names: Patricia Neal, actress; Patricia Hodge, actress; Patricia Routledge, actress; Patricia Highsmith, author.

Peggy. *See* MARGARET

Phemie. *See* EUPHEMIA

Philippa [fil-lip-pu]
Meaning: 'lover of horses'.
Feminine version of PHILIP.
Queen Philippa of Hainault (1314–69), wife of Edward II, was responsible for introducing the herb rosemary into England. She later led the English army against the invading Scots.
Diminutive: Pippa
Famous name: Philippa Gregory, novelist.

Philomena [fil-o-mee-nu]
Meaning: 'beloved' in Greek.
The name was used by early Christians of the Roman Empire, and has been popular in Scotland in the twentieth century.

In 1802 a tomb was discovered in a catacomb in Rome, closed with three tiles on which was painted an inscription in Latin, 'Peace be with you Philomena'. Inside were the bones of an adolescent girl, accompanied by a phial of blood, which in those days was accepted as a sign of martyrdom.
Variant spellings: Philomene, Filomena

Phyllis [fil-lis]
Meaning: 'foliage' or 'leafy branch' in Greek.
In Greek mythology, Phyllis died of love and changed into an almond tree after her death. The name increased in popularity in Scotland when Robert Burns wrote a song called 'Phillis the Fair'.
Variant spellings: Philis, Philliss, Phylis, Phyllys, Phylliss
Famous name: Phyllis Logan, actress.

Pippa. *See* PHILIPPA

Primrose [prim-rose]
Although it is one of the flower names so popular in Victorian times, it is thought that in Scotland it was originally a Scottish surname and later came to be used as a first name.

Rachel [rai-tch-el]
Meaning: 'ewe' in Hebrew.
It was probably used originally for its symbolic meaning of 'gentleness'.

In the Old Testament Rachel was the second wife of Jacob. Her tomb, which stands just outside Bethlehem, is venerated by Christians, Jews and Muslims. Like all Old Testament names, or names with biblical associations, it was popular in Scotland.

The Puritans used the name in the sixteenth and seventeenth centuries, and it became particularly popular in Scotland in the nineteenth century.
Variant spellings: Rachael, Racheal, Raquel, Rachalle
Gaelic cognate: Raonaid
Famous names: Raquel Welsh, actress; Rachel Roberts, actress.

Raonaid. *See* RACHEL

Rena. *See* ANDREW

Rhona [roe-nu]
Meaning: derived from the Norse *hraun-ey* (rough isle).
The origin of the name is a Scottish place name, Rona. It began to be used as a first name at the beginning of the twentieth century.
Variant spelling: Rona

Riona. *See* CATHERINE

Roberta [rob-ber-tu]
Meaning: 'fame' or 'bright' in Old German.
This is the usual feminine form of ROBERT in Scotland.

Variant spelling: Robertina.
Diminutives: Robyn, Robina, Robena
Famous name: Roberta Flack, singer

Robertina. *See* ROBERTA

Robyn. *See* ROBERTA

Rona. *See* RHONA

Rose [row-s]
Meaning: from the Gaelic *ros* or the Latin *rosa*.
Around the twelfth century, the Norman family de Ros, acquired land in various parts of Scotland, and a small Nairnshire clan became Rose of Kilravock. This must have influenced the name's usage in Scotland.
Diminutives: a great many diminutives and foreign forms of Rose have been used in Scotland, some of which are Rosalie, Rosaleen, Rosie, Rosanne, Rosina and Roslyn.
Gaelic cognate: Ros
Famous names: Dame Rose Macaulay, author; Roseanne Barr, actress.

Rowena [roe-ee-nu]
Meaning: from the Celtic for 'fair'.
In Sir Walter Scott's novel *Ivanhoe* (1819), Wilfred, Knight of Ivanhoe, loves Rowena, his father's ward. He rejects the more interesting Rebecca to marry her.

Ruth [rooth]
Meaning: 'friend' or 'companion' in Hebrew.
In the Bible Ruth was a Moabite woman who left her own family to remain with her mother-in-law, Naomi.

Afterwards she became the wife of Boas and the ancestress of David.

The name came to be used in Britain after the Reformation. It was used in the seventeenth century, especially among the migrating Puritans who, like Ruth, had also left their homes.

Ruthven, which has also been used as first name, was an aristocratic family name. After a treasonable conspiracy an act of Parliament was passed ordering the surname of Ruthven of be abolished. The ban was lifted in 1641.

Famous name: Ruth Prawer Jhabvala, author.

Ruthven. *See* RUTH

Sadie. *See* SARAH

Sara. *See* SARAH

Sarah [Sair-u]
Meaning: 'Queen' or 'Princess' in Hebrew.
In the Old Testament Sarah was the wife of Abraham. She gave birth to Isaac at the age of ninety.

This was a favourite name among the Puritans in the seventeenth century, and its meaning, combined with its religious connections, ensured its popularity in Scotland.
Variant spellings: Sara, Zara, Zarah
Diminutive: Sadie
Gaelic cognate: Sara (pronounced to rhyme with far)
Famous names: Sarah Bernhardt, actress; Sarah Miles, actress; Zara Phillips, daughter of Princess Anne.

Seasaidh. *See* JANET

Senga. *See* AGNES

Seona. *See* SHONA

Seonaid. *See* JANET

Seorsag. *See* GEORGINA

Sheena. *See* JANE

Sheila [shee-lu]
A phonetic form of the Gaelic name Sìle, which is a form of CECELIA.
Variant spellings: Shelagh, Shiela, Sheelagh, Sheelah, Sheilagh.

Famous names: Sheila Grier, actress; Sheila Hancock, actress; Shelagh Delaney, playwright.

Shona [sho-nu]
Meaning: 'God is merciful'.
The usual Scottish phonetic spelling of the Gaelic name Seonaid, a feminine form of JOHN.
Variant spellings: Shonag, Shonagh, Shonah, Shone
Gaelic cognate: Seona
Famous name: Shona Lindsay, actress.

Sile. *See* CECILIA and SHEILA

Sine. *See* JANE

Siusaidh. *See* SUSAN

Susan [soo-san]
Meaning: 'lily' in Hebrew.
Susannah is the fuller form of this name. It owed its popularity to the biblical story of Susannah and the Elders. Susannah had spurned the advances of the Elders and in their fury they made false accusations against her. Daniel interrogated the Elders and found that their stories contrdicted each other. They were put to death, the fate that Susannah would have suffered had their accusations been proved.
Variant spellings: Susannah, Susanna, Suzann, Suzanne
Diminutive: Sue, Susie, Suzie
Gaelic cognate: Siusaidh
Famous names: Susan Hampshire, actress; Susan Hayward, actress; Susannah York, actress; Susan Hill, novelist; Susan Sarandon, actress; Suzi Quatro, singer.

Susannah. *See* SUSAN

Suzanne. *See* SUSAN

Tamsin. *See* THOMASIN

Theresa [ter-ee-zu]
Meaning: probably from the Greek for 'inhabitant of Thera'.
Thera (or Thira, now Santorini) is an island in the Aegean
Sea which has experienced many volcanic eruptions over the
centuries. One of them may have given rise to the Atlantis
legend.

St Theresa of Avila was a popular saint of the sixteenth
century. After twenty-five years as a Carmelite, she founded
the convent of St Joseph in Avila in 1562 with thirteen nuns,
in conditions of poverty, hardship and solitude. This convent
became a prototype for others.

St Theresa of Lisieux lived an exemplary life as a
Carmelite nun. She died of tuberculosis in 1897, aged
twenty-four, leaving a short spiritual autobiography which
was translated into many languages and caused the
sensational spread of her cult.
Variant spelling: Teresa
Famous names: Mother Teresa of Calcutta; Teresa Braganza,
opera singer; Teresa Gorman, politician.

Thomasin [tom-as-een]
Meaning: 'twin' in Aramaic.
This is the medieval feminine form of THOMAS, which was
revived in the mid-nineteenth century as Thomasina.

One reason for the early use of Thomasin might lie in the
traditional belief that the apostle Thomas had a twin sister.
Variant spellings: Thomasena, Thomasina, Thomasine, Tamsin
Diminutive: Tammy
Famous name: Tammy Wynette, country and western singer.

Tricia. *See* PATRICIA

Uilleag. *See* WILMA

Una [oo-nu]
Meaning: from the Latin for 'one'.
This is the anglicized version of the Irish name Oona or
Oonagh. Una is the heroine of the first part of the *Faerie
Queene* (1596), Edmund Spencer's allegorical poem. After
many adventures, including escaping from a fiery dragon,
she is married to the Red Cross Knight.
Famous name: Una Stubbs, actress and television personality.

Ursula. *See* OSLA

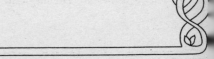

Vanora [van-or-u]
Meaning: 'white wave' in Celtic.
This is the Scottish equivalent of the name Guinivere.

Veronica [ve-ron-ee-ka]
Meaning: from the Latin meaning 'true image'.
St Veronica is said to have been the woman who wiped the face of Jesus with a cloth on his way to Calvary. According to legend his features remained as an image on the cloth she used.

James Boswell wrote that the name was introduced to his family in the seventeenth century through his Dutch grandmother Veronica, Countess of Kincardine.

Initially only used by Roman Catholic families, it came into general use in the mid-nineteenth century.
Variant spellings: Verona, Veron, Veronice, Vernice
Famous name: Veronica Lake, actress.

Violet [vy-oh-let]
Meaning: the name of the flower.
The use of this name originated in Scotland, probably due to the influence of the French name Violette.

In France, the violet was associated with Napoleon and worn by his followers as a secret badge while he was in exile. No doubt this helped the popularity of the name in Scotland.
Famous names: Violet Trefusis, lover of Vita Sackville-West; Violet Gordon Woodhouse, musician.

Vivien [viv-ee-en]
Meaning: derived from the Latin for 'lively'.
The girl's name is associated with Tennyson's poem 'Vivien and Merlin'. The magician, Merlin, fell in love with Vivien,

Lady of the Lake, who turned his magic against him and imprisoned him in a castle of air from which he could not escape.

Variant spellings: VIVIAN (also a boys name), Vivianne, Vivienne, Vyvien

Famous name: Vivien Leigh, actress.

Wilma [wil-mu]
A feminine version of WILLIAM, helmet of resolution, and the most popular form of Wilhelmina in Scotland.

William the Lion, as he was called because of his lion standard, succeeded his brother Malcolm IV in 1165. After extreme personal bravery he was defeated by the English, and became Henry's vassal.

Variant spellings: Williamina, Wilhelmina
Diminutives: Minna, Mina
Gaelic cognate: Uilleag

Zelda. *See* GRISELDA

BIBLIOGRAPHY

Brewers Dictionary of Names. London, Cassell,

Darton, Mike. *The Dictionary of Scottish Place Names*. Moffat, Lochar Publishing, 1990.

Dorward, David. *Scottish Surnames*. Edinburgh. The Mercat Press, 1992.

Dunkling, Leslie and Gosling, William. *Everyman's Dictionary of First Names*. London, J.M. Dent & Sons, 1991.

Dunkling, Leslie. *Scottish Christian Names*. Stirling, Johnson & Bacon, 1998.

Grimble, Ian. *Clans and Chiefs*. London, Blond & Briggs, 1980.

Hamilton, Gerald. *In Search of Scottish Ancestry*. London, Phillimore, 1972.

Hanks, Patricia and Hodges, Flavia. *A Dictionary of Surnames*. Oxford, Oxford University Press, 1988.

Hanks, Patrick and Hodges, Flavia. *A Dictionary of First Names*. Oxford, Oxford University Press, 1990.

Harrod, Jacqueline and Page, Andre. *The Bumper Book of Babies' Names*. Tadworth, Clarion, 1998.

Mackie, R.L. *A Short History of Scotland*. Edinburgh, Oliver & Boyd, 1962.

Maclean, Fitzroy. *Highlanders*. London, Adelphi, 1995.

Mitcheson, Rosalind. *A History of Scotland*. London, Methuen, 1970.

Moncreiff of that Ilk, Sir Iain. *The Highland Clans*. London, Barrie & Jenkins, 1982.

Morgan, Peadar. *Ainmean Chloinne: Scottish Gaelic Names for Children*. Isle of Skye, Taigh ne Teud Music Publishers, 1994.

Partridge, Eric. *A Dictionary of Traditional First Names*. Ware, Wordsworth Editions, 1951.

Powling, Suzy ed. *Choosing a Name for Your Baby*. London, Chancellor Press, 1993.

Saville, Jenny. *Babies' Names*. London, Ward Lock, 1987.

Scots Kith and Kin. London, Collins, 1989.

Sims, Clifford Stanley. *The Origin and Signification of Scottish Surnames*. Vermont, Charles E. Tuttle, 1969.

Sleigh, Linwood and Johnson, Charles. *Harrap Book of Boys' Names*. London, George G. Harrap & Co, 1962.

Sleigh, Linwood and Johnson, Charles. *The Book of Girls' Names*. London, George G. Harrap & Co, 1962.

Way, George and Squire, Romilly. *Scottish Clan and Family Encyclopedia*. Glasgow, HarperCollins, 1994.

Withycombe, E.G. *Oxford Dictionary of English Christian Names*. 3rd ed. Oxford, Clarendon Press, 1977.

Yonge, C.M. *History of Christian Names*. Gale, 1863.